"David Hesselgrave shaped evangelical missiology in the late twentieth and early twenty-first centuries. During the last months of his life, he penned *We Evangelicals and Our Mission*, a postscript that traces the history of evangelical missions in order to identify a modern crisis of doctrine and duty. The 'Dean of Evangelical Missiology' delivers one final lecture instructing evangelicals how to resolve this impending crisis by reviving historic doctrine and reengaging world evangelization."

—**Matt Queen**, Associate Professor and L. R. Scarborough Chair of Evangelism, Associate Dean of the Roy J. Fish School of Evangelism and Missions, Southwestern Baptist Theological Seminary

"David Hesselgrave, the dean of modern missiology, has produced a thoughtful, penetrating, and comprehensive examination of the foundations of the mission enterprise. *We Evangelicals and Our Mission* reviews the history of evangelicalism, defining and offering a solution to the problems of modern missions. . . . Every evangelical will benefit from reading this ground-breaking work that will stand the test of time."

—**Robin Dale Hadaway**, Senior Professor of Missions, Midwestern Baptist Theological Seminary

"Evangelical Christianity faces a crisis of identity. The greatest tragedy of this crisis is the way it erodes our missionary vision and zeal. We need to listen to the words of one of the greatest missiological thinkers of our time, David Hesselgrave. This book serves as a warning and provides correction for the church as we seek to maintain our focus on God's mission. This book will be an important contribution to evangelical missiological literature and serves as Dr. Hesselgrave's clarion call for us to stand strong and press forward for the glory of the God."

—**Scott Hildreth**, Assistant Professor of Missiology, George Liele Director of the Center for Great Commission Studies, Southeastern Baptist Theological Seminary

"Readers will find in *We Evangelicals and Our Mission* an abundance of wisdom, careful and thoughtful reflection, biblical conviction tethered to the best of the Christian tradition, and a heart for faithful witness and mission. . . . Evangelical theology, world evangelization efforts, and church ministry will be strengthened by the much-needed and timely appeal to reconnect missions and ministry to historic orthodoxy articulated so clearly in this volume. Highly recommended!"

—**David S. Dockery**, President of International Alliance for Christian Education, and Distinguished Professor of Theology, Southwestern Baptist Theological Seminary

"David Hesselgrave is perhaps the greatest missiologist of the last half of the twentieth century. Everything he has written is worth reading. *We Evangelicals and Our Mission* is no exception. Highly recommended."

—**Bruce Ashford**, Professor of Theology and Culture, Southeastern Baptist Theological Seminary

"David Hesselgrave died in 2018, but he still speaks wisdom to us today. I've always admired how Hesselgrave integrates theology and missiology. This book does the same, but the author adds church history to the mix, to the benefit of his readers. This book reminds me of 2 Timothy, Paul's last letter to his protégé. Hesselgrave warns his readers of theological dangers to missions and champions prioritism. I enthusiastically recommend this book."

—**John Mark Terry**, Emeritus Professor of Missions, Mid-America Baptist Theological Seminary

"The familiar tones of scholar, missionary, and prophet are on full display in this latest Hesselgrave volume. In many ways it continues his thoughts and exhortations from earlier works. Readers will be struck by Hesselgrave's clear definition of evangelicalism and his compelling vision to reintegrate evangelicalism by unabashedly retethering it to the Bible, the great tradition, and an evangelistic thrust within our Great Commission efforts. This book is invaluable for the church and the academy."

—**Greg Mathias**, Associate Director of Center for Great Commission Studies, Assistant Professor of Global Studies, Southeastern Baptist Theological Seminary

"At a time when everything is considered missions, even if the gospel is never shared, this book serves to remind and refocus the reader on the Great Commission task. Hesselgrave and Davis have done a noble work describing the relationship between present activity and history and belief. If you want a summary of where evangelicals have been, and potentially where we are going, read this book!"

—**J. D. Payne**, Professor of Christian Ministry, Samford University

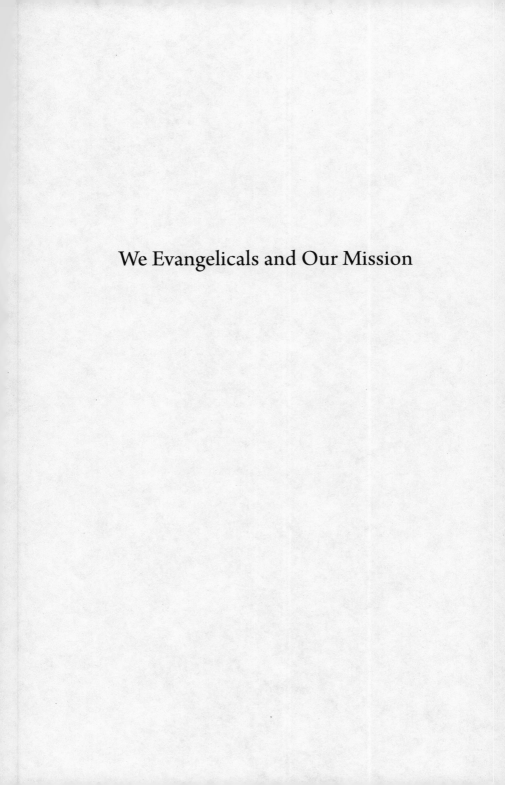

We Evangelicals and Our Mission

We Evangelicals
and Our Mission

*How We Got to Where We Are and How
to Get to Where We Should Be Going*

David J. Hesselgrave
WITH Lianna Davis

FOREWORD BY
Keith E. Eitel

 CASCADE *Books* · Eugene, Oregon

WE EVANGELICALS AND OUR MISSION
How We Got to Where We Are and How to Get to Where We Should
Be Going

Cascade Books
An Imprint of Wipf and Stock Publishers
199 W. 8th Ave., Suite 3
Eugene, OR 97401

www.wipfandstock.com

PAPERBACK ISBN: 978-1-7252-7128-9
HARDCOVER ISBN: 978-1-7252-7127-2
EBOOK ISBN: 978-1-7252-7129-6

Cataloguing-in-Publication data:

Names: Hesselgrave, David J., author. | Davis, Lianna, author. | Eitel,
Keith E., foreword.

Title: We evangelicals and our mission : how we got to where we are and
how to get to where we should be going / by David J. Hesselgrave and
Lianna Davis ; foreword by Keith E. Eitel.

Description: Eugene, OR: Cascade Books, 2020 | Includes bibliographi-
cal references.

Identifiers: ISBN 978-1-7252-7128-9 (paperback) | ISBN 978-1-7252-
7127-2 (hardcover) | ISBN 978-1-7252-7129-6 (ebook)

Subjects: LCSH: Evangelicalism | Missions | Evangelistic work | Evan-
gelicalism—United States

Classification: BV2063 H47 2020 (print) | BV2063 (ebook)

Manufactured in the U.S.A.   09/15/20

Dedicated to Carl F. H. Henry, Kenneth Kantzer,
and Robert Culver

Contents

Illustrations and Tables

Foreword

ONE FORMER STUDENT RETURNED from mission work in Jordan and presented me with a beautiful, hand-woven carpet depicting a scene of a train of camels in a caravan. Then he told me the story behind the carpet, which enhanced the meaning of the gift. An old man, ninety-five years old or so, was blind and wanted to teach his great-grandson the art of weaving such carpets. It took six months sitting closely behind his great-grandson, whispering in his ear thread by thread what to weave when and where to depict the beautiful scene upon completion. The old man could not see, but in his mind's eye, he could see clearly because he had woven that pattern thousands of times and could recall every step from memory.

This imagery shows the concern of an elder generation for a younger one to relay a lifetime of knowledge and wisdom. It establishes the historical context, defines motion, and surfaces meaning to a process. We as evangelicals have witnessed the passing of an elder generation of missiologists. We are the grandchildren and great-grandchildren listening as one generation whispers into our ears theological and missiological wisdom, meaning, and purpose.

Such is the book in hand. David J. Hesselgrave became a dear friend as he mentored me through my doctoral work at the Trinity

Evangelical Divinity School in the 1980s. I have highly valued his whispers ever since. He spoke with great learning, good historical understanding, and yet he did so with grace and humility. His words will ring true as you read. He wove together the threads of numerous theological traditions, and their impact on missions thinking, that have appeared over the last 500 years or so. That weave created a fine image of analysis and thoughtful critique that was always tethered to stable, inerrant truth from God himself and whispered into the ears of those eager to listen to things that are of eternal significance.

Four distinct patterns are outlined in this book. First, Hesselgrave sets evangelicals into the context of great traditions of thought, from the Reformation forward. Second, he demonstrates the trajectory of ecumenical thought as it intersected that of the evangelical traditions and altered them along the way. Third, controversial issues surface the ways evangelicals have wrestled with the intersection of ecumenical thought, and Hesslegrave cogently argued the issues with biblical conviction and reason. Finally, he points the reader to the significance of all these trends for the future of evangelicalism specifically and Christianity in general.

To demonstrate Hesselgrave's keen sense of need to whisper in the ears of another generation, he invited his granddaughter, Lianna Davis, to write a concluding essay from the distinct point of view of a millennial. She carefully and transparently speaks of her own theological journey having lived life around her grandfather's influence and her tussles of faith and understanding as she too studied in college and seminary. Her contribution shows she also sat weaving as the elder whispered into her ear the strands of thought from a wise grandfather.

Hesselgrave is gone now. Yet, his wisdom will sound loudly for at least another generation or two. To those of us touched by his weave of words, it will continually ring in our ears until we join him in eternity.

Keith E. Eitel

Preface

WHAT HAPPENED TO THE church? The founder of Public Religion Research Institute (PRRI) provides some answers in his *The End of White Christian America*. Many erstwhile attendees of mainline denominations will indicate agreement. Evangelical answers will tend to be mixed, but it will perhaps surprise you how many will respond in terms of their particular experience and the "way things are going" in the church they attend now. Not all evangelicals have the larger picture in mind, especially when North America is in view.

Kregel Publications published my book *Paradigms in Conflict: 10 Questions in Christian Missions Today*. A second edition, enlarged and enhanced by contributions from a number of well qualified and well-known missiologists, is scheduled to be released this summer (2018). My chapters and most of the additional chapters in this second edition are given over to biblical analysis of important missions/missiological questions.

First, for reasons that will become apparent, this follow-up book complements *Paradigms in Conflict*—one might almost say is a companion to *Paradigms* in that it is *not* about "*biblical* analysis" but rather "historical analysis." Second, it is also anecdotal, not in the sense that it highlights missionary stories, but in the sense that it highlights missionary/missiological relevance. All of Christian history has relevance and importance for Christianity(!), but some of it has special importance for evangelical mission/missiology. That is our special focus here.

I want to express profound appreciation to my granddaughter, Lianna Davis, for accompanying me over these last two hundred pages of history and commentary. She is a graduate student, wife of Tyler Davis (an actuary in the life insurance industry), and mother of two daughters. She is conservative but contemporary, and she and Tyler have been helpful in keeping me informed of current evangelical thinking and doings in missions. Without their help in summarizing, along with other endeavors, this book—short as it is—may have proved impossible.

Finally, I want to express gratitude to my son-in-law, Marty Kroeker, who helped to finalize the text.

Prolegomenon

ALMOST TWO THOUSAND YEARS after the coming of Christ and approaching five hundred years since the Reformation, two highly-placed Anglican clerics decided to debate the "essentials" of evangelical Christianity![1] Liberal David L. Edwards, provost of London's Southwark Cathedral and former editor of the prestigious SCM Press, and evangelical John R. W. Stott, rector emeritus of All Soul's Church in London and former chaplain to Her Majesty the Queen, were at odds on some of the most basic and defining doctrines of the Christian faith. Pressed by his protagonist, Stott ultimately resorts to some quite crude but illuminating metaphors to illustrate the fundamental difference between the evangelicals and liberals. He writes,

> [The liberal] seems to me to resemble (no offence meant!) a gas-filled balloon, which takes off and rises into the air, buoyant, free, directed only by its own built-in navigational responses to wind and pressure, but entirely unrestrained from earth. For the liberal mind has no anchorage; it is accountable only to itself.
> The Evangelical seems to me to resemble a kite, which can also take off, fly great distances and soar to

1. Edwards and Stott, *Evangelical Essentials*.

great heights, while all the time being tethered to earth. For the Evangelical mind is held by revelation. Without doubt it often needs a longer string, for we are not renowned for creative thinking. *Nevertheless, at least in the ideal, I see Evangelicals as finding true freedom under the authority of revealed truth, and combining a radical mind and lifestyle with a conservative commitment to Scripture.*[2]

This book is all about the difference between liberal "gas-filled balloons" and evangelical "kites" viewed in terms of Stott's metaphors: (1) the "stake" of authoritative Scripture, (2) the "tethers" of doctrinal/creedal statements that tie beliefs and behaviors to Scripture, and (3) the "cords" (or "strings") that evangelicals employ to control evangelical "kites" of witness and work (my elaboration of Stott's phrase "tethered to earth").

2. Edwards and Stott, *Evangelical Essentials*, 106 (emphasis mine).

Part I: **Evangelicals and the Great Tradition of Christian Thinking**

A DECADE OR SO ago, Trinity Evangelical Divinity School (TEDS) published a Festschrift in honor of church historian John D. Woodbridge entitled *The Great Commission: Evangelicals and the History of World Missions.*[1] In the Festschrift, Trinity's associate professor of church history and the history of Christian thought, Douglas A. Sweeney, provides several definitions of "evangelical" as offered by scholars of other schools and backgrounds. He then offers a stipulated definition of his own. Each of the definitions/descriptions has something to commend it, but in this book, I prefer to adopt and adapt Sweeney's definition because it is grounded in church and mission history. He says,

> I prefer to describe evangelicalism with more specific-
> ity as a movement that is based on classical Christian
> orthodoxy, shaped by a Reformational understanding
> of the gospel, and distinguished from other such move-
> ments in the history of the church by a set of beliefs and
> behaviors forged in the fires of the eighteenth-century
> revivals—the so-called "Great Awakening" . . . —beliefs

---

1. Sweeney, "Introduction." See also, Sweeney, *American Evangelical Story*, 82.

and behaviors that had mainly to do with the spread of the gospel abroad.[2]

I agree. I believe that the "stakes," "tethers," and "cords" of classical orthodoxy; the Reformation understanding of the gospel; and Great Awakening beliefs and behaviors including missions/missiology reflect what the evangelical movement and its mission should be if it is to have a future (Figure 1). It goes without saying that I cannot do justice to the whole of that history. I probably will not do justice to all that Sweeney has in mind, and for that I apologize. I ask the reader to think of what follows in Part I as no more than a series of snapshots of the history involved and to do his or her own study to fill in the gaps of which there will be many.

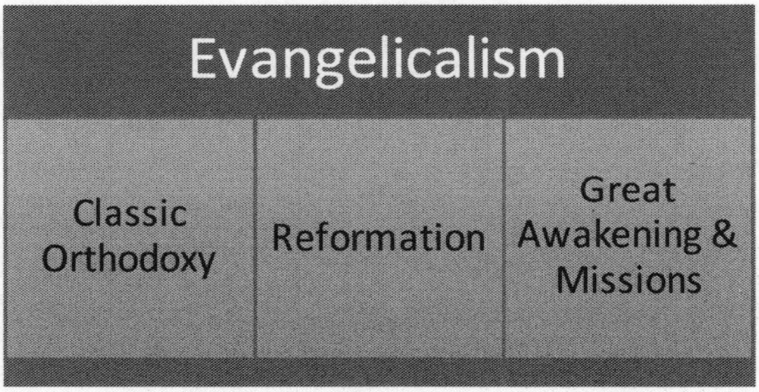

Figure 1. Three sources of Evangelicalism

Of the many references that undergird Part I, a little book on the great tradition coauthored by David Dockery and Timothy George and published by Crossway has been most helpful to my purpose.[3] Of the words used in the title of that book the one most likely to give pause to some readers is the word "tradition." However, Dockery and George quote the Methodist scholar Thomas Oden, who says, "All that is meant by tradition, then, is the faithful handing down from generation to generation of scripture interpretation consensually received worldwide and cross-culturally

2. Sweeney, "Introduction," 2.
3. Dockery and George, *Great Tradition.*

through two millennia."[4] Oden's phraseology is worth pondering—"scripture interpretation," "consensually received," "worldwide and cross-culturally," "handed down through two millennia." That is precisely what we are attempting to discover here, and it is not only good, it is "essential to evangelicalism."

4. Oden, *Rebirth of Orthodoxy*, 32.

Chapter 1

"Based on Classical Christian Orthodoxy"

ACKNOWLEDGING A SPECIAL DEBT to Douglas Sweeney's historically oriented definition of what it means to be evangelical on the
one hand, and what has proved to be a complementary study of
The Great Tradition of Christian Thinking by David Dockery and
Timothy George on the other, we begin our study with the early
church and the apostolic fathers. With the completion of the earthly
ministry of the Lord Jesus and his return to the Father, where did
they find true doctrine and divine direction? Paul answers that
question in large part when, addressing the church at Thessalonica,
he admonished believers to "stand firm and hold to the traditions
that you were taught by us, either by our spoken word or by our
letter" (2 Thess 2:15). The Christian great tradition begins with the
inspiration and inscripturation of the word of God and proceeds
with its proclamation, dissemination, and instruction.

The Scripture Canon: The Old and New Testaments

Wherever the Christian faith has been found, there
has been a close association with the written Word of
God, with books, education, and learning. Studying
and interpreting the Bible became natural for the early

5

> Christian community, having inherited the practice
> from late Judaism.[1]

The great tradition is not only rooted in the biblical text itself but also in the history of the study and interpretation of the biblical text. It shows that, historically, Bible interpretation was informed by approaches inherited from intertestamental Judaism and the Graeco-Roman world of the apostles. However, with the passing of the apostles various needs surfaced: the need for an authoritative Scripture canon, the need to clarify and defend apostolic beliefs and practices, the need to encounter and counter false religionists, the need to reply to heresies within the church, and the need to respond to persecution from without the church. In one form or another—and to one or another degree—these challenges continued and were met by the church throughout the classical period and beyond.

The single most important part of the Christian Tradition is, of course, the New Testament itself.[2] Jesus promised that the Holy Spirit would bring what he had taught them to the minds of the apostles and "guide them into all truth" (John 16:13). That promise was extended so as to include the apostle Paul and Luke the historian. Scholars disagree as to the date of the pastorals, Peter's epistles, Hebrews, James, Jude, and the Gospel of John, but it is safe to say that by the end of the first century or very shortly thereafter the early church possessed at least a good part of the New Testament and accorded it the authority that went with apostolic authorship. With that authority and additional agreements among the churches, the New Testament canon essentially as we have it today was accepted by the churches before two more centuries had passed. *That Bible came to be our Bible and with it came the true truth and undivided authority that forever attends the word of God.*

The apostolic witness contained in the writings of the apostles, then, was the authoritative source for addressing key issues

1. Dockery and George, *Great Tradition*, 23.

2. Or, perhaps better, the New Covenant because that links the New Testament with the covenantal character of God's relationship with Israel and with covenant theology as well.

that faced the early church. The following table summarizes these issues and key figures and events in the second through the fifth centuries of the church.

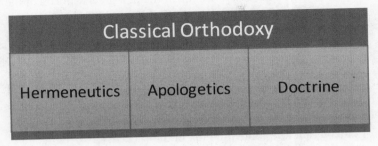

Figure 2. Three main elements of classical orthodoxy

Hermeneutics: Interpreting and Applying the Written Word

Following the death of the apostles, and as the church moved into the second century, more attention was given to ways of understanding and applying Scripture to everyday life and thought. Which books and letters are authentic? How is the New Testament to be understood? What is the relationship of New Testament books to the Old Testament? Marcion (ca. 85–160) and the gnostics abandoned the Old Testament and interpreted the New Testament according to their own ideas. Justin Martyr linked the testaments with each other, both being an outgrowth of the Logos. Toward the end of the second century Irenaeus and Tertullian improved on the understanding of Justin and also stressed the mutuality of both testaments and theological tradition.[3] Two schools of interpretation were most influential.

3. Cf. Dockery and George, *Great Tradition*, 26–29.

The School at Alexandria

Origen (185–254), who studied under Clement (ca. 150–215) of the school at Alexandria, was one of the first great scholars of the church and a leader of a catechetical School of Alexandria. In *First Principles* Origen systematized the rules of faith and distinguished between "necessary" doctrines delivered by the apostles and other doctrines. He believed that Bible interpretation must of necessity follow the rule of faith including the doctrines of God, Christ, and the Holy Spirit; the doctrine of spiritual beings including angels and Satan; and the doctrine of last things such as the reward of the righteous and the condemnation of the wicked.

Origen's work represented a response to the interpretations of Marcion and the gnostics and thus met a growing need of the church during the early centuries. However, Origen went beyond the teachings of the apostles in maintaining that the Scriptures are subject to a threefold interpretation. "For as man is said to consist of body, and soul, and spirit, so also does sacred Scripture" he wrote.[4] Accordingly, he concluded, there is the literal or historical meaning which corresponds to the body; the moral sense or higher stage or meaning corresponding to the soul; and, finally, the highest sense of all corresponding to a man's spiritual nature. Only by allegorizing the Bible in this way can we "enter into its Holy of Holies," said Origen.[5] However, Origen's fanciful hermeneutic was rejected by the early church.

The School at Antioch

It remained for the School of Antioch, represented by men such as Theodore of Mopseustia (ca. 350–428) and John Chrysostom (354–407), to develop an improved method of Bible interpretation for the church—a method less given to Platonic imagination and more in-line with Aristotle's "down-to-earth" orientation. Antiochene hermeneutics decried allegorical interpretation and

4. Origen, *Princ.* 4.1.11 (776).

5. Williams, *Early Church Fathers*, 106.

replaced it with typological interpretation in which the events, people, and things of the Old Testament are understood as prefiguring or foreshadowing the events, people, and things of the New Testament. Theodore also gave increased attention to the historical record and to the overall purposes of God as revealed in the Bible. As for Chrysostom, he "gave primary attention to the literal, grammatical and historical interpretation of Scripture."[6]

> The Alexandrians looked to the rule of faith, mystical interpretation, and authority as sources for shaping the Christian intellectual tradition. The Antiochenes looked to reason and the historical development of Scripture as the focus for understanding Christian thought. These approaches set the stage for the widely influential and shaping work of Augustine.[7]

Apologetic and Polemic Writings

In the last part of the second century and throughout the third centuries it became increasingly apparent that "Christians had to fight what every strategist tries to avoid—a war on two fronts."[8] While Christians were dealing with false teaching and heresy from within the church, they were forced to deal with harassment and persecution from outside the church as well. Williston Walker writes,

> The charges brought against Christians, not to mention the official policy of treating the church as an unauthorized association, impelled believers not only to bear witness in suffering but also to explain and defend their faith. There arose, therefore, in the course of the second century a new genre of Christian literature, the "apology"—so called from the Greek *apologia*, meaning "a speech for the defense." The authors of these works are known collectively as the apologists; and though writings of this type were produced long after the close of the

6. Dockery and George, *Great Tradition*, 35.

7. Dockery and George, *Great Tradition*, 35.

8. Cairns, *Christianity through the Centuries*, 97.

second century, the period from about AD 130 to about 180 is frequently referred to as the age of the Apologists.[9]

Early apologists included Quadratus, Aristides, Melito, Athenagoras, Theophilus, Irenaeus, Tertullian, and Justin Martyr. Justin Martyr, who seems to have headed up a school in Rome, wrote one of the most famous early apologetic works, entitled simply *Apology*. One of his disciples, Tatian, wrote *Discourse to the Greeks*—a work that was as much a polemical attack on pagan culture and religion as it was a defense of Christianity. Irenaeus (born around AD 130) is sometimes known as the "Missionary Bishop." His best-known apologetic work is *Against Heresies*, though he himself called it *An Examination and Overthrow of What Is Falsely Called Knowledge*—a title that was most apt since the book was largely directed against Gnosticism and the gnostics. Finally, Origen presented the gospel as the final goal of man's quest for truth and defended it against all detractors. Among his six thousand writings of various genres, *First Principles* and *Against Celsus* are usually considered to be his best works.

Confessions and Creeds

As noted above, the church was called upon from within as well as without to make her faith known, and that she did with increasing unity and clarity right up to the triumph of Constantine. In fact, in some ways that was even more true after Constantine intruded his secular power into the affairs of the church. In such a context, it is easy to lose sight of the profound importance of creeds and confessions that serve to articulate and confirm the faith of the true Christian. These early confessions took two basic forms: 1) rules of faith and 2) classic creeds.

9. Walker et al., *History of the Christian Church*, 53. See also Ott et al., *Encountering Theology of Mission*, xxiv.

Table 1. Rules of faith and classic creeds

Term	Basic Meaning
Rules of Faith	Essential or core beliefs of "early church laity."
Classic Creeds	Standardized or universal creeds adopted in response to theological controversies.

"Rules of Faith"

Rules of faith were confessional statements or core beliefs of the "early church laity."

> Christians sought to maintain religious unity by a rule of faith which, beginning with simple forms, gradually acquired more precise and definite expression; it was in essential points the same everywhere and was impressed upon all Christians at baptism.[10]

Classic Creeds

The Apostles' Creed, the Nicene Creed, and the Creed of Athanasius are often classified as the "Three Universal Creeds."[11] After the persecuted church was reconciled to the state under Constantine in 313, seven major councils (among others) were called to resolve disruptive—and often, contentious—theological controversies. Nicaea (325) introduced a new stage in creedal development. At Nicaea an "ecumenical council adopted a creed that was to be a test for orthodoxy and was to be authoritative for the whole church."[12]

It is important to be aware of the kind of issues with which early major councils had to do, such as the relation of Christ to

10. Baus, *History of the Church*, 151.

11. Hanegraaff, *Christianity in Crisis*, 375.

12. Leith, *Creeds of the Churches*, 28.

the one God as well as the means and method of man's salvation. About 318, a presbyter from Alexandria named Arius asserted that Jesus was of a similar but lesser essence or substance than God—*homoiousios* (of like substance) but not *homoousios* (of the same substance). Apolinarius basically agreed. He held that the Christ of Bethlehem and Nazareth—and of Calvary and the Empty Tomb—was not fully man. Docetists, on the other hand, held that Christ was entirely too divine in his nature to suffer either pain or death. He only *seemed* (Greek *dokeo*) to do so. All of these proposals were wrong, but they were more than wrong; they were heretical. And they were answered with increasing completeness and clarity at councils at Nicaea in 325, Constantinople in 381, and the Council of Chalcedon in 451: Christ is, at one and the same time, fully God and fully man.

As concerns man's salvation, the idea that man is lost and in need of salvation was seldom questioned. Rather, the fathers attempted to explain the work of Christ in redeeming mankind. J. N. D. Kelly suggests that running through all the various attempts to explain Christ's redemptive work was "one grand theme"—recapitulation—derived from the apostle Paul by Irenaeus and presupposed in sacrificial theory. It held Christ to be

> representative of the entire race. Just as all men were somehow present in Adam, so they are, or can be, present in the second Adam, the man from heaven. Just as they were involved in the former's sin, with all its appalling consequences, so they can participate in the latter's death and ultimate triumph over sin, the forces of evil and death itself. . . . All of the fathers, of whatever school, reproduce this motif.[13]

In 409 a British theologian named Pelagius appeared in Rome and promoted the idea that humans are born with a free will and with the ability to understand and "cooperate" with God in overcoming evil and attaining salvation and righteousness. Among others, Augustine argued against Pelagius, holding tenaciously to

13. Kelly, *Early Christian Doctrines*, 377.

the doctrines of original sin, human depravity, the sovereignty of God, and the gospel of grace.

In this respect as in many others, we are greatly indebted to the brilliant Augustine. "Augustine's work has shaped the best of the Christian intellectual tradition like few others during the two thousand year history of the church."[14] Most famous perhaps for writings such as *Against the Skeptics* and *The City of God*, multitudes of students will remember him best for works that relate to their special interests and needs. In my case that work would be his *On Christian Doctrine*—a work on hermeneutics sometimes thought to be the church's first volume on homiletics. In *On Christian Doctrine* Augustine rethinks his rhetorical learning in Alexandria and characterizes it as "gold from Egypt," but he makes it clear that its particulars must be examined to ascertain whether or not they are real gold. And he makes it clear that the amount of Egyptian gold available to preachers and teachers of the gospel is meager as compared to the gold to be found in the Bible.

Closing Reflections

Christians have been living in the light afforded by the apostles, early believers, and church fathers for two thousand years and more. For the most part Christians have taken what they have been given but with relatively little thinking and even less thanks; nevertheless, that heritage is inestimable. Enabled by the ministries of Christ and the Holy Spirit, those early believers accomplished a missionary task of inestimable proportions. Acknowledging a debt to Dockery and George, here are just a few aspects of the "deposit of faith" those early believers bequeathed to us:

- "Apostolic guidance"—studying and interpreting the Bible[15]
- Building on certain common commitments to Jewish tradition[16]

14. Dockery and George, *Great Tradition*, 38.
15. Dockery and George, *Great Tradition*, 23.
16. Dockery and George, *Great Tradition*, 24.

- The Bible as primary source for shaping the Christian tradition[17]

- In time the "church had to demonstrate on biblical grounds that the same God was revealed in both Testaments"[18]

- A "pattern of Christian truth"—the integration of faith and reason[19]

All of this and more lay behind the faith consensus that the church of the classical period bequeathed to the church of subsequent ages. Viewed from a missionary perspective, it is more than the church of any age could have dreamed, much less anticipated. A paragraph from the writings of the eminent missions historian, Bishop Stephen Neill, sums it up well.

> Inwardly, the church had gone far to consolidate its life and to perfect its organization. It had defined the limits of the Scriptures, and had given to the New Testament equal canonical status with the Old. Through the work of the great Councils it had settled many questions of doctrine, and had laid down the limits within which Christian thought has moved ever since. . . . In the great Councils it had developed a marvelous instrument for the expression and maintenance of Christian unity; in spite of troublesome disputes as to the relative status and authority of the patriarchs—Antioch against Alexandria, and at times Rome against all the rest—Christians in every part of the world felt themselves to be at one with all other Christians.[20]

Somewhere[21] I recall a missions historian adding that missions history is usually told in terms of individuals and groups who left home and journeyed to distant places and peoples to share the

17. Dockery and George, *Great Tradition*, 24–25.

18. Dockery and George, *Great Tradition*, 25.

19. Dockery and George, *Great Tradition*, 52.

20. Neill, *History of Christian Missions*, 52.

21. I believe it was also from Stephen Neill although I can no longer find the passage.

gospel and build the church. It is seldom told in terms of theologians and ecclesiastics who defended the faith, instructed the church, and formed creeds and confessions that tethered the gospel to scriptural revelation. Nevertheless, those contributions are monumental and deserving of undying gratitude and careful study.

Chapter 2

"Shaped by a Reformational Understanding of the Gospel"

IN HIS BOOK *THE Light in Dark Ages*,[1] V. Raymond Edman shows that, though the Dark Ages were indeed dark, they were not without light. Having produced the likes of Clement and Augustine earlier, in the Dark Ages the church produced the likes of Ambrose, Bernard of Clairvaux, Thomas Aquinas, and Pascal. Then, as Europe emerged from the Middle Ages, the church also produced the likes of John Wycliffe, John Hus, and Girolamo Savonarola. With luminaries such as these, we begin the story of another part of the great tradition.

As ordinarily viewed, the Protestant Reformation began in AD 1517 when Martin Luther nailed his ninety-five theses to the door of the chapel in Wittenberg. However, church historians often differentiate between the "Old Protestantism" of leaders such as Waldo, Wycliffe, Hus, and Savonarola and the "New Protestantism" of the Reformers themselves. That distinction pushes "Protestant" beginnings back as far as the fourteenth and even the thirteenth centuries. That is important to Free Church historians especially, but also to theologians/missiologists generally, because the contributions of

1. Edman, *Light in Dark Ages.*

these "Old Protestants" to the "Reformational understanding of the gospel" are incalculable. The following table summarizes the three main strands of the Protestant Reformation.

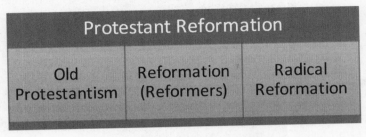

Figure 3. Main movements of the Protestant Reformation

The "Old Protestantism"

A complete accounting of the "Old Protestantism" would necessarily include contributions of mystics, humanists, and various church councils of the Middle Ages, but for our present purpose, we note only those ideas and movements that were set in motion by the four men noted above.

Peter Waldo (1140–1218) and the Waldenses

Following his conversion in 1170 and a trip to Palestine shortly after that, Peter Waldo gave all his property to his wife and the poor and gave himself unreservedly to asceticism and the study and preaching of the Bible. An appeal for papal recognition denied, his "Poor men of Lyon" were driven out of Lyon and migrated to southern Europe. There they became known for more than the vow of poverty; they also became known for denying the efficacy of the sacraments and repudiating indulgences, purgatory, and masses for the dead.

John Wycliffe (1330–84), the "Morning Star of the Reformation"

A student and then professor at Oxford, John Wycliffe at first thought to reform the Roman Church from within. Unsuccessful in that endeavor, from 1379 he began to oppose the dogmas of the church as well as the office and authority of the pope himself. Wycliffe insisted that Christ, not the pope, is head of the church; that the Bible, not the church, is the measure of true teaching; and that Christ is *spiritually* present in the bread and wine but not *substantially* present. By 1382 he had made the New Testament available to English readers in their own tongue. And though Wycliffe himself was condemned by the church, lay preachers who followed him—the Lollards—preached his message throughout England.

John Hus (1373–1415) and His Moravian and Pietist Successors

John Wycliffe's ideas contributed to the Peasants' Revolt in Germany but were also foundational to the work of John Hus (ca. 1373–1415) in Bohemia (Czechoslovakia). Hus was rector at the University of Prague and a leader of dissenting believers in Bohemia. He attempted to reform the Roman Church from within in accordance with the teachings of Wycliffe. As a consequence, he was summoned to the Council of Constance with a promise of safe passage by the church. Nevertheless, in 1415 he was condemned by the council, incarcerated in a foul dungeon, and summarily executed.

Less than fifty years after Hus's martyrdom, his followers organized the *Unitas Fratrum* or Unity of Brethren on the basis of four basic principles:

1. The Bible is the only source of Christian doctrine.

2. Public worship is to be modeled after that of the apostolic church.

3. The Lord's Supper is to be defined in biblical language and received in faith.

4. The essential evidence of true saving faith is true Christian living.

Despite almost incessant persecution, the Unity of Brethren movement grew in numbers and strength in Bohemia and Moravia. And it was Moravian migrants who, in 1722, found their way to the estate of Nicolaus Ludwig Zinzendorf (1700–60) in Saxony. Zinzendorf was a godson of Philipp Spener and a student of August Francke—two great Pietists and proponents of missions. He opened his *Herrnhut* (The Lord's Watch) estate to them, and together they spearheaded one of the greatest missionary forces of the eighteenth and nineteenth centuries.

Girolamo Savonarola (1452–98) and Reform Efforts within the Roman Church

Back in Italy, Savonarola entered the Convent of San Marco at age thirty and was later assigned to that city. He became one of the most prominent among those who tried their utmost to reform the church while remaining devoted to the church and its future. In the early 1490s Savanarola began preaching against the vile practices of the church as well as the world. He pleaded for repentance and purity, and he warned of judgment if his message went unheeded. His preaching actually produced a significant religious and moral revival, but he ran afoul of the pope, was excommunicated, and then executed in 1498.

The "Reformation Reformers"

Coming to the Reformation itself, it is not overly difficult to mark out its major features and personnel. But it is as much or more to the point here that we highlight the doctrinal and spiritual progression that gave impetus to the formation of the "Reformation gospel" in order to both satisfy Sweeney's definition of Evangelicalism and to underscore the critical importance of that formation.

Martin Luther (1483–1546)

Five hundred years ago on October 31, 1517 Martin Luther posted his ninety-five theses on the door of the Castle Church in Wittenberg. It is not just in the substance of those theses (almost wholly given to the evils of selling indulgences) but also in the act of nailing them to the church door that one understands something of the man Martin Luther.

Like Augustine, Luther was sensitive to his need for forgiveness of sin and a need for salvation from boyhood days. His father wanted him to study law, but in 1505 he joined the Augustinian order and became a student at the university in Erfurt. There he both studied and taught until 1511 at which time he was transferred to the University in Wittenberg where he served until his death in 1546. The story of those years can be told in terms of inner cognitive and outer theological/ecclesiastical controversies that constitute his life experience. For example,

1. It was during his tenure as lecturer in theology that he and some of his colleagues first became aware of, and committed to, the doctrine of justification by faith that was the lynchpin of the Reformation understanding of the gospel.

2. When preparing lectures on the Psalms, Romans, Galatians, and Hebrews, Luther's theology became grounded in Rom 1:17 and in the conviction that only by a commitment to the authority of Scripture alone and only by faith in the Christ of the Bible could one be justified before a holy God.

3. The ninety-five theses directed against Tetzel's sale of indulgences were nailed to the door of Castle Church in Wittenberg in 1517. This was only the beginning of a controversy that lasted for years and entailed Luther's growing conviction that separation from the Roman Church was the only way to establish the biblical ideal of the church.

4. After a debate with Johannes Eck in Leipzig in July 1519, Luther became increasingly aware of the opposition of the Papacy and civil authorities. It was then that he published the paper "The Babylonian Captivity of the Church" and other papers attacking the church hierarchy and sacramental practices. Threatened with excommunication by the Curia, a papal ban was placed on him and confirmed by imperial authority at the diet of Worms in May 1521. Luther refused to recant, and a reformation started that could not be stopped.

5. In 1525 Luther repudiated his monastic vows and married Katherine Von Bora with whom he fathered six children. For this he was roundly criticized, but Katherine Bora's table became a center of theological and spiritual training for numerous students who regularly found their way to that fellowship.

It should be mentioned that rationalists such as Erasmus—originally a supporter of Luther—had little sympathy for the doctrine of justification by faith. Erasmus held that reform would come by education, by the rejection of superstition, and by a return to ethics rather than by doctrinal dogmatism. This was the challenge at one extreme of the philosophical/theological spectrum. At the other extreme, mystics and/spiritualists such as Karlstadt accused Luther and Lutherans (and Romanists as well) of being "scribes" who suppressed the "inner word" in slavish dependence upon the biblical text. For Karlstadt, the truth of the Bible was subject to the test of religious experience.

As for Luther himself, early on he relied on allegorical interpretation but later abandoned it in favor of historical and Christological interpretation. In a word,

> Martin Luther broke the stronghold of fanciful interpretation with his commitment to *sola scriptura*, which stressed not only the primacy of Scripture but also the historical sense of Scripture as the true and only sense

that provided a sound framework for thinking Christianly about God and his world.[2]

Philipp Melanchthon (1497–1560)

In 1518 at the age of twenty-one, Philipp Melanchthon joined the faculty at Wittenberg as professor of Greek. He was proficient in the classical languages and of a like commitment to Reformation issues. Possessing a gentle demeanor, Melanchthon proved to be of unrivalled value as the "theologian of the Reformation."

In his writings and actions Melanchthon contributed to the Reformation cause for more than thirty years. He accorded more authority to Scripture than to the church and the fathers. His faith was essentially Reformed theology. Among his numerous writings were *Loci Communes*, a short overview of the theology of his colleagues at Wittenberg. His theological works were designed to encourage lay persons to study the Bible. It was he who bore the major responsibility for the formation and publication of the Augsburg Confession.

John Calvin (1509–64)

Educated in literature and law, John Calvin experienced a "sudden conversion" in 1532. The ultimate result was that he became a fugitive from his native France and settled in Geneva. Banished from Geneva for a time, he returned in 1541 and remained there until his death in 1564.

Calvin is justifiably known as the great systematizer of Reformed theology. Calvin's greatest work was *The Institutes of the Christian Religion*, the first edition of which was small and completed in 1536. Its subject matter had to do with the Ten Commandments, the Christian faith as based on the Apostles' Creed, prayer as understood from the Lord's Prayer, the sacraments of baptism and the Lord's Supper (including a discussion of the evils

2. Dockery and George, *Great Tradition*, 45.

of the Roman views), and Christian liberty. By the time a final edition was published in 1559, it was a major text on theology and comprised four books and eighty chapters![3]

Assigning a lesser role to revelation in nature and reason, Calvin assigned supreme authority to Scripture interpreted under the guidance of the Holy Spirit. Believers are to acknowledge Scripture as having the same authority as if they had heard the words uttered by God himself. It was from a completely authoritative Bible that Calvin became convinced of the total sovereignty of God. From that doctrine flowed much of his theology, including his famous "five points" and his acceptance of the church, the sacraments (baptism and the Lord's supper), and civil government as divine institutions. Citing Augustine, Calvin affirmed that man is by nature depraved, that faith in Christ is the foundation of salvation, and that repentance leads to regeneration and the restoration of the divine image.[4]

Like Luther, Calvin believed that the office of an apostle was temporary and that the apostles had no successors. But, while Calvin basically agreed with Luther as far as the office and role of the apostles is concerned, he also believed that it is God's will that the gospel be preached to all people. As a consequence, the only Protestant mission outside of Europe in the sixteenth century was the Calvinist mission to Brazil in 1555. Surveying Calvin's theological system, Roger Greenway says that, as it relates to mission, three truths stand out: the glory of God as primary goal, the all-embracing doctrine of the kingdom of God, and the doctrine of the sovereignty of God.[5]

Due to Calvin (and also to Zwingli), the Reformed Church expanded, and Reformed theology spread rapidly on the Continent and then across the Channel to Great Britain. Reformed

---

3. Cairns, *Christianity through the Centuries*, 310.

4. Luther agreed, but held on to the notion that Christ could be present anywhere and in any form he desired (i.e., ubiquitous) and was in that sense present in the elements of the Lord's Supper. Calvinists staunchly disagreed, arguing that was too close to Catholic doctrine of transubstantiation.

5. Greenway, "Calvinism," 155.

ecclesiology worked its way out not only in the formation of national Reformed Churches in France and Holland, but in the Presbyterian and Reformed churches of Scotland and England and other countries. Reformed theology also worked its way out in the theology of Dutchmen such as A. Saravia, G. Voetius, and J. Heurnius, and later on, in the thinking of Americans such as J. Eliot, D. Brainerd, and J. Edwards. In England it was reflected in the Edwardian Homilies (1547) which were read in the churches and included Thomas Cranmer's "Of the Salvation of All Mankind," sometimes said to be one of the finest pieces of theological writing in the English language. Finally, confessionally it worked its way out a hundred years later in the Westminster Confession written in London in 1646. The Westminster Confession set the standard for Presbyterianism, including the Presbyterian missions of the entire English-speaking world.

Ulrich Zwingli (1484–1531)

Prior to Calvin's arrival in Switzerland, Reformed churches had their beginnings under Ulrich Zwingli and others. Zwingli advocated a reformation of government as well as of the church itself. Believing that it was the duty of those in authority to rule in the name of Christ, he held that civil governors should also rule in the church. Theologically, like Luther and Calvin, Zwingli was basically Augustinian, but his theology was less rigid than that of the former and less systematic than that of the latter.

Reformation Councils, Creeds, and Confessions

One consequence of theological ferment in the Reformation period was that, as John Leith says, "the Reformation ushered in a new era in creed-making."[6]

---

6. Leith, *Creeds of the Churches*, 61.

Lutheran Churches and Lutheran Confessions

Though Luther himself deplored the name "Lutheran," his followers not only adopted the name but thought it to be essential that Lutherans codify their doctrines. This they did in *The Small Catechism* and the Augsburg Confession (mentioned above) and dating to 1529 and 1530 respectively. *The Small Catechism* was the work of Luther and grew out of his concern for theological literacy among Lutheran laity. It began with an exposition of the Decalogue, the Apostles' Creed, and the Lord's Prayer, and it dealt with other matters soon to be covered more authoritatively in the Augsburg Confession.[7] The Augsburg Confession itself was largely the work of Melanchthon. It represented a singular effort, first to "establish the integrity of the Christian faith of the Protestants" on the basis of the Scripture; and, second, to correct abuses in the life of the church.[8]

About thirty years after the death of Luther, *The Formula of Concord* (1577) represented an attempt to resolve differences within Protestantism in general and within Lutheranism in particular. The *Formula* contained the three great universal creeds of the early church and various Lutheran creeds drawn up over the preceding half century. It made Lutherans especially conscious of the importance of doctrine, but it also tended to entrench a cold, scholarly orthodoxy to which Pietists and others reacted.[9]

Calvinistic Reformed Churches and Reformed Confessions

It is instructive to note that Calvin's famous *Institutes* noted above was originally an apology for the Reformed faith as well as a polemic directed against the Roman Church. More specifically, it was addressed to Francis I of France and represented an attempt to defend persecuted Protestants and, as well, to "urge Francis to accept

7. Leith, *Creeds of the Churches*, 107–26.

8. Leith, *Creeds of the Churches*, 63.

9. Cairns, *Christianity through the Centuries*, 297.

the ideas of the Reformation."[10] Only over time was it developed into the theological tome that we know today.

The Lutheran and Reformed streams and confessions basically agreed with each other, but with a difference in emphasis. According to Philip Schaff,

> the Lutheran Confession starts from the wants of sinful man and the personal experience of justification by faith alone, and finds, in this Article . . . comfort and peace of conscience, and the strongest stimulus to a godly life. The Reformed Churches (especially the Calvinistic section) start from the absolute sovereignty of God and the supreme authority of his holy Word and endeavour to reconstruct the whole Church on this basis. The one proceeds from anthropology to theology; the other, from theology to anthropology.[11]

The "Radical Reformation"

If the Lutheran and Reformed streams were basically complementary to each other, there were two important Protestant streams that arose about the same time and were much less inclined to agree with each other: the "right wing" Anabaptists in Germany and the "left wing" Puritans in England.

Anabaptists in Germany and Switzerland

By the beginning of the sixteenth century, evangelical congregations (i.e., those that claimed to be reformed in accord with the gospel) were rapidly forming in many regions of Germany and also in Switzerland. As yet, however, they had no fixed constitution or order of service. In Luther's Germany a leading light among them was the Anabaptist preacher Thomas Muenzer. Muenzer was executed in 1525 at the close of the Peasants' War, but, after the

10. Cairns, *Christianity through the Centuries*, 310.

11. Schaff, *Creeds of Christendom*, 235.

re-baptism of the Catholic priest Menno Simons in 1535, followers of Muenzer and Simons became known as "Menno's followers"
or Mennonites. Anabaptists were divided and diverse. But they
always exhibited a general distrust of external authority, rejected
infant baptism, and espoused pacifism, non-resistance, and the
common ownership of property. Seeing the church as a "counter-
community" and withdrawing from ecclesiastical bodies to which
they belonged, Anabaptists characterized the church as the "visible
embodiment of the kingdom of God" which contains only those
who are truly citizens of that kingdom. Some historians refer to the
Anabaptist movement as the "radical Reformation."

Separatists, Nonconformists, and Puritans in England

Gradually but surely, Free Church sentiments and movements developed in most countries that had state churches. Earle Cairns,
for example, chronicles the way in which the Scottish church's efforts to maintain Presbyterian polity and Calvinistic theology were
threatened by autocratic kings and liberal clerics for over a century
after ridding itself of Catholic control in 1567.[12] Soon afterwards,
in England, "Separatists," "Nonconformists," and "Puritans" alike
objected strenuously to a 1582 Parliament decision that deemed it
treason to worship outside the Church of England. Considerably
later, in 1646–47, the Westminster Confession encouraged con-
gregationalism and buttressed the Free Church movement. As far
as the movement itself is concerned, it was not until the founding
of America and especially after the passage of the Bill of Rights
in 1791 that the separation of church and state became a widely
accepted political principle and that free, independent churches
came to be widely understood and accepted.

12. Cairns, *Christianity through the Centuries*, 403–4.

"An Understanding of the Gospel": The Reformation Heritage in the Great Tradition

Very much unlike "classical period orthodoxy," the "gospel under-standing of the Reformation" seems to be near at hand and more readily understood. However, the Reformation story is very complicated and does not readily admit of a simple telling, though we must try to do just that.

The Reformation Gospel as Part of "the Great Tradition of Christian Thinking"

In his book *The Story of the Reformation* William Stevenson includes a chapter entitled "Our Reformation Heritage" in which he succinctly summarizes the influence of the Reformation on the whole of the Western world.[13] However, after dealing with economic, political, and social advances he writes, "The lodestar of the Reformers was neither economics nor politics nor even social amelioration but *religion first and last and all the time*."[14] Stevenson then quotes the well-known liberal Paul Tillich to the effect that "Protestantism is not *only* Protestantism, it is also— and first of all—Christianity."[15]

How very true. By placing an open Bible in the hands of the people, by emphasizing the authority of the Bible, by providing public worship in the language of the people, by encouraging family worship, by making the preaching of the word indispensable, "the Protestant Reformation was instrumental in advancing personal religion, it was also, for that very reason, a means of promoting the Kingdom of God on earth."[16]

It is a misunderstanding to see Reformation theology in terms of its political effects. Once again, the Reformation was "religion first and last and all the time." Dockery and George break

---

13. Stevenson, *Story of the Reformation*, 177–85.

14. Stevenson, *Story of the Reformation*, 178 (emphasis mine).

15. Stevenson, *Story of the Reformation*, 182.

16. Stevenson, *Story of the Reformation*, 185.

that down into two great principles of the Reformation: formal principles and material principles.[17]

The Formal and Material Principles of the Reformation

Dockery and George are very much to the point when they write,

> Luther, Calvin, along with Ulrich Zwingli and other Reformation and Post-Reformation thinkers, contended that the Scripture must be believed, rightly interpreted, applied, and experienced to truly and redemptively advance the Christian intellectual tradition.[18]

Later in their book, they differentiate between the *formal* and *material principles* of the Reformation.

Table 2. Formal and material principles of the Reformation

Term	Meaning
Formal principal	*sola scriptura*, God's word alone
Material principal	*sola gracia/fide*, justification by grace alone through faith alone

The formal principle is what is meant by *sola scriptura*, and concerning it, Luther said,

> We are determined by God's grace and aid to abide in God's Word alone, the holy Gospel contained in the biblical books of the Old and New Testaments. This Word alone should be preached, and nothing that is contrary to it. It is the only Truth. It is the sure rule of all Christian doctrine and conduct. It can never fail or deceive us.
>
> Whoso builds and abides on this foundation shall stand against all the gates of hell, while all merely human

17. Dockery and George, *Great Tradition*, 74.
18. Dockery and George, *Great Tradition*, 46.

editions and vanities set up before it must fall before the presence of God.[19]

The material principle refers to the doctrine of justification by faith alone.

> Building on the anti-Pelagian thrust of the Augustinian tradition, the Protestant Reformers emphasized that no one can be made righteous before God through the piling up of merits, the intercession of the saints, or human works of any kind. *Salvation is by grace alone, through faith alone, in Jesus Christ alone.* This was not seen as a novel teaching or new doctrine suddenly come to light in the sixteenth century. The Reformers saw themselves in doctrinal continuity with the early church when they set forth the material principle of the Reformation.[20]

Closing Reflections

Theologians refer to two kinds of faith and often differentiate them by two Latin expressions: *fides quae*, or "the faith that we believe" and *fides qua*, "the faith by which we believe."

Laypersons make the same or a very similar differentiation when they sing "Faith of our Fathers, Holy Faith" on the one hand, and "My Faith Looks up to Thee, Thou Lamb of Calvary" on the other. One kind of faith is objective—the kind that Jude says we are to contend for (Jude 3). The other kind of faith is subjective—the kind to which Paul was referring when he told the Philippian jailer to "believe on the Lord Jesus Christ and you shall be saved" (Acts 16:31).

Something similar needs to be said regarding grace (Greek *charis*). Etymologically and theologically *charis* has two sides or ingredients: the unmerited favor or gift of God on his part and the thankful reception of his favor or gift on the part of humans.

19. Dockery and George, *Great Tradition*, 74.
20. Dockery and George, *Great Tradition*, 74 (emphasis mine).

Both are necessary for salvation and, indeed, for relating to God in Christian living.

It can be said in a variety of ways, but it should be repeated a thousand times, especially at a time in history when so many are thinking and working diligently to dull or even erase the doctrinal lines between Protestantism and Catholicism. Given the official pronouncements and commitments of the Catholic Church, the more obscure and unidentifiable those lines become, the more obscure and unidentifiable becomes the saving gospel.

Chapter 3

"Beliefs and Behaviors Forged in the Fires of Eighteenth-Century Revivals"

IT IS QUITE NATURAL to focus on three great mission efforts that came out of the eighteenth century. The first was the *Unitus Fratrum*, the Moravian Church that settled *Herrnhut* in Saxony. Under the leadership of von Zinzendorf they began their foreign mission outreach in 1732 and soon became one of the most productive mission churches of history. Humanly speaking, their success can be credited to von Zinzendorf's leadership, to their missionary passion, and to a strategy that quickly resulted in the formation of churches in target areas.

The second locus of missionary sending, of course, was Great Britain, commencing with the sending of William Carey and his colleagues at the end of the eighteenth century and culminating in what K. S. Latourette terms the "Great Century" in Protestant missions, also known as the "British Century." Carey's insistence that the Great Commission is applicable to the church today played a significant role in that sending as did the British revivals that accompanied the labors of the Wesleys and their Methodist colleagues.

Thirdly, almost universally known though not always mentioned is the fact that many if not most of the first settlers in the colonies of the New World came in pursuit of freedom of worship. Not so well known is the fact that some came to minister to both colonists and "heathen" Indians. The first of the thirteen colonies to be settled (1607) was Virginia. The Virginia Company charter actually called for the "spread of the gospel among the heathen," but that missionary effort did not go well. In the northern colonies it went better. Upon landing at Plymouth Rock in 1620 the pilgrims set apart one of their number to promote the conversion of the Indians. In 1628 Charles I granted a charter to Massachusetts which stated that "the principal end of the plantation was the conversion of the Indians."[1] As early as 1636 the General Court of Massachusetts ordered ministers to appoint two of their number each year who would undertake missions among the Indians. Early on, missions were undertaken at Martha's Vineyard and Nantucket. Five generations of one missionary family, the Mayhews, labored at Martha's Vineyard. Known as the Apostle to North American Indians, John Eliot came to Massachusetts from Cambridge in 1630 and served as both pastor to a Presbyterian church and missionary to Indians. Before he died thirty years later he had translated the Bible into Mohican, published a number of books including theological books, and helped establish groups totaling 3600 believers in fourteen settlements.

Surrounded by "heathen" Indians, it took some time before colonial churches undertook a "sending abroad." That time did come, however. Attendant with ministerial and missionary efforts both north and south was the establishment of colleges for the training of Christian youth. Harvard (1636), William and Mary (1693), Yale (1701), and other colleges were founded with the specific purposes of educating youth morally and religiously as well as training ministers of the gospel.

Kenneth Scott Latourette writes that, eventually, "the Christianity of New England molded the entire United States and had repercussions which were felt the world around."[2] Such is the

---

1. Kane, *Christian Missions*, 95.
2. Latourette, *Three Centuries of Advance*, 194.

background to our consideration of the Great Awakening and, eventually, the "spread of the gospel abroad."

Figure 4. Sources of Evangelicalism in the eighteenth century

Firebrands of the Great Awakening

Though the First Awakening began small, it soon erupted into a spiritual conflagration that swept over broad areas of the country. Jonathan Edwards regarded it as a veritable miracle of grace bestowed by a Sovereign God even though he himself did not live long enough to see its full extent either in time or territory.[3] All Christians today—though with varying degrees of knowledge and appreciation—think and live in light provided by the Great Awakening and its storied leaders.

Theodore Frelinghuysen

It was the pietistic preaching of Theodore Frelinghuysen, a Dutch Reformed pastor in New Jersey, that was instrumental in igniting revival fires in the Middle Colonies in 1725 to 1726. Arriving as a new pastor in 1719, Frelinghuysen was appalled at the spiritual and moral state of his congregation. Without celebrity status and without fanfare, he preached so as to lead congregants to repentance, salvation, and holy living. Though opposed by some members of his own church, revival nevertheless broke out in the church and spread first to Scotch-Irish Presbyterian congregations

3. Hatch et al., *Gospel in America*, 139–40.

pastored by Gilbert and William Tennent Jr. Somewhat later, promoted by Jonathan Edwards, revival broke out among New England Congregationalists. By the time the revival peaked in 1740 to 1742, it had spread beyond New England congregations to Presbyterians in Virginia, Baptists in North Carolina, and Methodists in Maryland and Virginia.

Jonathan Edwards

Pastor, theologian, missionary, and college president, Jonathan Edwards was of good Puritan stock, especially on his mother's side. Her father, Solomon Stoddard, was pastor of the prestigious Congregational Church in Northampton, Massachusetts. Blessed with exceptional parentage, Jonathan Edwards was a precocious student and one of the most brilliant philosopher-theologians America has ever produced. Today his intellect and achievements are sometimes denigrated because his beliefs are so controversial. In addition, he is often perceived to have been a ranting preacher of fire and brimstone—largely because of his famous sermon "Sinners in the Hands of an Angry God." Truth told, however, Edwards's theology was extremely well thought-out, and he was not given to ranting or pulpit-pounding. He actually read "Sinners in the Hands of an Angry God" in measured tones, and its content was strictly biblical.

As an upholder and supporter of the Great Awakening, Edwards was often criticized in his day among his peers for promoting the excessive behaviors connected with the revival even though those behaviors were beyond his control. Edwards's own spirituality exhibited a remarkable balance between rationality and experience. In any event, Jonathan Edwards first became an assistant of his grandfather, Solomon Stoddard, in 1727 and later succeeded him as pastor of the Northampton Church when Stoddard died in 1729. In 1735, during the revival that marked his ministry in Northampton, Edwards wrote,

> The Spirit of God began to be so wonderfully poured out
> in a general way through the town, people had soon done
> with their old quarrels, backbitings, and intermeddling
> with other men's matters. The tavern was soon left empty.
> Every day seemed in many respects like a Sabbath day.[4]

Founders of the Northampton church had largely been converted from the world. Such was not the case with the succeeding generation, so Stoddard had provided for a "Half-Way Covenant" according to which unconverted people who had been baptized as infants were allowed to unite with the church though they were not allowed to vote or participate in the Lord's Supper. Edwards opposed the Half-Way Covenant and, after years of discussion and debate, was put out of his prestigious Northampton pulpit in 1750. His farewell sermon displayed no animosity, although Edwards was heartbroken. His text was "2 Corinthians 1:14, and his emphasis was on what would happen when ministers meet their congregations at the future judgment."[5]

Edwards and his family moved to Stockbridge, Massachusetts, in 1751. There, with very limited resources and while ministering cross-culturally to nearby Indians, Edwards wrote some of his most important theological works along with a biography of David Brainerd, premier missionary to the Indians. He was named president of Princeton in 1757 and took office a year later. However, a smallpox vaccination (some say he submitted to the vaccination as part of an experiment) caused an infection and resulted in his death that same year.

George Whitefield

Critical to the character and course of the Awakening in America—and linking it to the Evangelical Revival in Great Britain—were the ministries of George Whitefield and John (and Charles) Wesley. Whitefield was a strict English Anglican Calvinist who,

---

4. Edwards, "Faithful Narrative," 177.

5. Wiersbe, *10 People Every Christian Should Know*, 22.

nevertheless, had been greatly influenced by the Wesleys. Making seven trips to America between 1738 and 1770, Whitefield's evangelistic ministry crossed denominational and doctrinal boundaries and attracted huge crowds. Thousands gathered

> to hear him speak in the most stirring terms about the "New Birth." . . . [He] spoke of his ecumenical hopes for a "revival of true and undefiled religion" in all religious groups. Promote revival he would, though in a "catholick spirit" that was decidedly Calvinist in tone and aimed especially at listeners who would be moved by the rhetoric of total human depravity and supernatural grace.[6]

On one preaching tour of New England in 1740 Whitefield preached 130 sermons in seventy-three days. When he preached his farewell sermon in Boston before returning to England, twenty thousand people came to hear him.[7] After cooperating with all phases and expressions of the First Great Awakening and giving himself unreservedly to the promotion of it for the better part of a generation, Whitefield died during his final visit to America in 1770, physically exhausted from his spiritual exertions over many years.

John Wesley

Not noted as a leader of the Great Awakening in America, the visits and influence of John Wesley merit something more than a mere mention. Like Edwards, Whitefield was a Calvinist. The Wesleys, of course, were Arminian. Nevertheless, both the Wesleys and Whitefield were Anglicans who experienced evangelical conversion—John Wesley by reading Luther's commentary on Romans concerning justification by faith, Whitefield by reading a book given to him by Charles Wesley entitled *The Life of God in the Soul of Man*. Whitefield began "field preaching" in 1739 and asked Wesley to do the same in Bristol that same year. Both the Wesleys and Whitefield emphasized open-air preaching, used lay

6. Stout, "Great Awakening," 495.
7. Hatch et al., *Gospel in America*, 139–40.

preachers, organized converts into societies, and initiated social enterprises of various kinds; this in spite of the fact that Whitefield and Wesley were at odds with each other theologically. Whitefield remained staunchly Calvinist while, over time, Wesley became increasingly Arminian. In fact, their differences on election and free grace were significant enough to bring about a parting of the ways as early as 1740. Their differences were not allowed to sever either their friendship or their support and participation in the Awakening, however. In 1770 John Wesley was selected to preach George Whitefield's funeral sermon in London.

The Beginnings of Modern Protestant Missions in England and America

There is, of course, much more to be told. Much of it has to do with England. The misunderstanding tends to persist that William Carey and his colleagues were more or less alone and unaided in launching and sustaining the missionary effort in that country. That view ignores the influence of the evangelical revival that stirred the upper class in the Anglican Church between 1790 and 1830. Nevertheless, William Carey is rightly known as the "Father of the Modern Protestant Missions," and it would be difficult to overstate his missionary contribution in England as well as in India.

William Carey and Missions in England

It was May 31, 1792. The modern missionary movement was to be born that day, but only God himself knew that to be the case. Certainly none of the Christians gathered in Nottingham chapel that day had much inkling of it. Most of them were quite convinced that when a sovereign God wanted the gospel taken to "heathen" in the far-flung continents and islands of the world, he would see to that. They themselves were quite content to do little or nothing.

It was at such a time and place that a self-educated shoe cobbler by the name of William Carey preached one of the most memorable and influential missionary sermons of all time. Ascending the pulpit Carey read his text, Isa 54:2–3, and began to speak. At issue, he said, is "the world." Over and over again, biblical texts refer to "the world." "What are we to do about 'the world?'" he asked.

> "Lengthen thy cords"—so ran the text—"*lengthen thy cords and strengthen thy stakes, for then shalt break forth on the right hand and on the left; and thy seed shall inherit the Gentiles and make the desolate cities to be inhabited.*"
>
> "*Lengthen thy cords!*" said the text.
>
> "*Strengthen thy stakes!*" said the text.
>
> "*Expect great things from God!*" said the preacher.
>
> "*Attempt great things for God!*" said the preacher.
>
> "If all the people had lifted up their voices and wept," says Dr. Ryland, "as the children of Israel did at Bochim, I should not have wondered at the effect; it would only have seemed proportionate to the cause; so clearly did Mr. Carey prove the criminality of our suppineness in the cause of God!" But the people did not weep! They did not even wait! They rose to leave as usual. When Carey, stepping down from the pulpit, saw the people quietly dispersing, he seized Andrew Fuller's hand and wrung it in an agony of distress. "Are we not going to *do anything*?" he demanded. "Oh, Fuller, call them back, call them back! We dare not separate *without doing anything!*" As a result of that passionate entreaty, a missionary society was formed, and William Carey offered himself as the Society's first missionary.[8]

As far as Carey's ministry in India is concerned, there are those who look at the tremendous accomplishments of the Serampore Trio and especially Carey in translating not only the Bible but Indian classics, in preparing a dictionary, in managing an indigo factory, in representing locals before British authorities, and so on that they more or less assume that his view of missionary

---

8. Boreham, "William Carey's Life Text," paras. 8–10 (emphasis in original).

work was inclusive and that all of these and other efforts qualified as being part of the Christian "mission." That is not the case.

Given the opportunity to speak before the Governor General and his full court at the age of forty-three, Carey relayed not the improvements and benefits his presence had upon the community. Instead, the registered indigo planter vindicated his position as a missionary with a statement evoking Luke's report of Paul's brief time in Athens (Acts 17:17): "I have been in the habit of preaching to the multitudes daily, of discoursing with the Brahmins upon every subject, and superintending schools for the instruction of Hindu youth."[9]

Samuel J. Mills and the Society of the Brethren in America

Across the Atlantic in the new nation of America, contrary winds were blowing—winds emanating from the French Revolution, from British deism, and, especially, from the Enlightenment. So much so that in 1798, the General Assembly of the Presbyterian Church stated "The eternal God has a controversy with this nation."[10] By that time some churches had been turned into riding stables or houses of prostitution, Bibles had been burned, and not a few pastors had been killed, especially on the frontier. Some of the schools founded for the training of preachers had been abandoned or secularized. At one of them, Yale College, "Few students professed regeneration. Gambling, profanity, vice, and drunkenness were common among students, who were proud of being infidels."[11]

As the seventeenth century gave way to the eighteenth, that decline caused deep and widespread concern both in and out of the church. Another great movement of the Spirit of God became essential if the faith of the fathers and the Reformers was to be recovered. Moved by the state of the new nation and inspired by still-glowing embers of the First Great Awakening, denominational

9. Walker, *William Carey*, 195–96.
10. Mansfield, *Lincoln's Battle with God*, 16–17.
11. Cairns, *Christianity through the Centuries*, 417.

leaders urged believers to pray that people would once again return to God. Pray they did. And God answered with the beginnings of a Second Great Awakening and with a grand vision for taking the gospel to the "heathen" nations of the world.

The Second Awakening is often said to have begun as a revival in Hampden-Sidney College in Virginia in 1786. But within a few years there were revivals at other schools as well—Washington College in the south and Yale, Williams, and Dartmouth in the north. In 1802 and as a direct result of the fervent Bible preaching of college president Timothy Dwight (1752–1817), about one-third of the student body at Yale professed conversion.[12] From there the revival progressed to other colleges and through three interconnected phases to New England, upstate New York, and on the frontier.[13]

It's a story often told but not told often enough. In 1802, one Samuel Mills was called to preach the gospel to the nations while he was plowing on the family farm in Connecticut. Four years later as a student at Williams College in Williamstown, Massachusetts, he and a group of kindred spirits formed the Society of the Brethren. One day, when going to a place of prayer, they sought shelter from a sudden storm in the lee of a haystack and prayed for the "heathen world." Then they stood to their feet and said, "We can do it if we will."

Several of those students went on to study at Andover Newton, a new school founded by "Old Calvinists" and bearing the imprint of Jonathan Edwards. Andover-Newton became a fountainhead of both New England Evangelicalism and the American missionary movement abroad. At Andover-Newton, Mills, Gordon Hall, and Luther Rice were joined by Adoniram Judson, Samuel Newell, and Samuel Nott Jr. Together they formed the Society of Inquiry on the Subject of Missions. Their entreaties resulted in the formation of the (American) Board of Commissioners for Foreign Missions. The first business of the new board was to respond to these candidates and their desire to be sent abroad.

12. Cairns, *Christianity through the Centuries*, 417.
13. Fitzmier, "Beecher, Lyman," 123–24.

Foreign missions proved to be complicated. But on February 6, 1812, Judson, Newell, and Nott (all three attended by their wives) along with Hall and Rice were ordained in the Tabernacle in Salem, Massachusetts. Two weeks later the Judsons and Newells set sail from Salem. The others sailed from Philadelphia on February 24.

A Legacy of "Beliefs and Behaviors Forged in Eighteenth-Century Revival Fires"

Generally speaking—and in spite of opposition—the revivals of the eighteenth and nineteenth centuries left an awareness among Christians that, very often, there is need for a fresh working of the Holy Spirit in both the church and society. Unsaved and unchurched people need to repent of unbelief and wrong living, be converted, and live righteous lives. Church members need either to repent and trust Christ rather than church membership and sacraments for salvation, or they need to recommit themselves to holiness and Christian living.

Timothy George draws special attention to the kind of legacy that supports this tradition.[14] Namely,

1. "A literature of gospel expectation"—tracts and books that were both challenging and hopeful for evangelization and revival efforts around the world. Examples would be Jonathan Edwards's *An Account of the Life of the Late Reverend David Brainerd*;[15] Jonathan Edwards's *An Humble Attempt to Promote Explicit Agreement and Visible Union of God's People, in Extraordinary Prayer, for the Revival of Religion, and the Advancement of Christ's Kingdom on Earth, Pursuant to Scripture-promises and Prophecies Concerning the Last Time*;[16] and

---

14. George, "Evangelical Revival," 51.
15. George, "Evangelical Revival," 47.
16. George, "Evangelical Revival," 48.

William Carey's *An Enquiry into the Obligations of Christians to Use Means for the Conversion of the Heathens.*[17]

2. "A theology of mission that guided the course of the missions movement." With reference to the applicability of the Great Commission, the First Great Awakening "posed a hermeneutical crisis" for those who had accepted the view that the commandment had been given to the apostles and their immediate successors and was no longer binding on the contemporary church.[18] Carey and others in the missionary movement challenged this view vigorously and with some success.

Nevertheless, their "new theology of mission" allowed "Wesleyans and Calvinists to cooperate in the task of world evangelization despite their different understandings of the divine decrees, predestination, perseverance and the other 'distinguishing doctrines of grace,' as Andrew Fuller called them."[19] This "new theology of mission" was summarized in six short statements by Fuller in his *The Gospel Worthy of All Acceptation* which was published in 1785:

- Unconverted sinners are commanded, exhorted, and invited to believe in Christ for salvation.

- Everyone is bound to receive what God reveals.

- The Gospel, though a message of pure grace, requires the obedient response of faith.

- The lack of faith is a heinous sin which is ascribed in the Scriptures to human depravity.

- God has threatened and inflicted the most awful punishments for their not believing in the Lord Jesus Christ.

- The Bible requires of all persons certain spiritual exercises which are represented as their duty.[20]

17. George, "Evangelical Revival," 49.
18. George, "Evangelical Revival," 50.
19. George, "Evangelical Revival," 51.
20. George, "Evangelical Revival," 51–52.

3. "An ecumenical spirit that enabled the theology of mission to flourish." Before the end of the eighteenth century, Isaac Watts's hymn "Jesus Shall Reign Where'er the Sun" with its millennial overtones had become a classic, Jonathan Edwards's *Humble Attempt* had inspired Baptists in the Midlands to organize the famous Prayer Call of 1784, Philip Doddridge of Northampton had set forth a plan for quarterly prayer meetings throughout England, and the Pietists and Moravians had demonstrated exemplary obedience and cooperation. But there is more. In the words of Timothy George,

> Precisely one hundred years after Carey had proposed such a gathering, the first international mission conference convened in Edinburgh in 1910. Evangelicals today who, *often with good reason, are suspicious and dismissive of the modern ecumenical movement* should not forget that the modern quest for Christian unity was born on the mission field. It sprang from the godly desire of Bible-believing Christians to take seriously the words of Jesus which directly connect the visible oneness of His followers on earth with the mandate He gave to them to evangelize in His Name.[21]

Closing Reflections

In conclusion, it is not too much to say that in some ways Great Awakening revivals tipped American Protestantism on its head. They resulted in an ecclesiastical democratization—in a bottom-up rather than a top-down Protestantism in which the laity as much as the clergy assumed authority in church life. Following the model of the federal government and its adoption of the new Constitution after the close of the War for Independence and precedents set by Methodists and Anglicans, more and more churches made up their own constitutions and created national churches. Unlike Old World Protestantism, the New World

21. George, "Evangelical Revival," 37 (emphasis mine).

Protestantism would feature denominationalism and the formation of religious movements—including evangelical Christian
movements—whose authority resided with "ordinary" believers.
For Evangelicals, faith statements and spiritual experience—especially a saving knowledge of and right relationship with Jesus
Christ—would generally be recognized as crucial to evangelical
belief and behavior. Though both continue to be crucial, it is the
relative importance of statements of faith on the one hand and
Christian experience on the other that have proved to be most
divisive in evangelical theology, evangelism, and mission. But that
is grist for the mills of a later chapter, as we shall see.

Part II: Ecumenism and Evangelicalism in Modern Times: An Overview

THERE WAS NOT JUST one, there were two great ideological movements in the eighteenth century. One—the Great Awakening—was a movement of the Spirit of God, redemptive and renewing. As Sweeney says and as we have confirmed, it resulted in evangelical beliefs, evangelical behaviors, and the "spread of the gospel abroad."[1] But there was another movement as well—the Enlightenment. The Enlightenment was, as Dockery and George say, "a watershed in the history of Western civilization."[2] It not only elevated nature, reason, science, and the arts to a new plateau in civic life; in so doing it also precipitated the rise of a new genre of theology and apologetic—theological liberalism. Far from encouraging the *recovery* of traditional Christian beliefs and classic apologetics, liberalism advocated the *refashioning* of those beliefs into a new religion that would be more acceptable—and even appealing—to "enlightened," "civilized," and "cultured" people East and West.

And so we enter the nineteenth and twentieth centuries—K. S. Latourette's "revolutionary age."[3] According to Latourette,

1. Sweeney, "Introduction," 2.
2. Dockery and George, *Great Tradition*, 47–48.
3. Latourette, *Christianity in a Revolutionary Age*.

Important though Christianity has been and is in the history of mankind, it is being vigorously challenged. In the past two centuries such large-scale open defections from it have occurred in its erstwhile stronghold, Europe, the traditional Christendom, that some thoughtful and even friendly observers have held that beginning at least as far back as the eighteenth century the world has been entering the post-Christian era.[4]

Why, Latourette asks, undertake to write a projected five volumes on a "dying faith"? Because the *faith* is not dying! The nineteenth century was the century in which "Christianity first became worldwide."[5] If anything was in its death throes it was *Christendom*, not *Christianity*—it was Christianity's sociopolitical influence that faded, not Christianity's "once-for-all-delivered-to-the-saints" *faith*!

---

4. Latourette, *Christianity in a Revolutionary Age*, 1:vii.

5. Latourette, *Christianity in a Revolutionary Age*, 1:viii. Latourette's "Great Century of Protestant Missions" begins with the end of the Napoleonic Wars of 1815 and ends with the outbreak of World War I in 1914.

Chapter 4

The Great Century and the Gathering Storm

THE CLOSING YEARS OF the nineteenth century and the open-
ing years of the twentieth made clear the fact that the gospel
had not just *spread* around the world, but its missionary bearers
had indeed gained ground. This gain was not just territorially,
they had gained ground in many other ways as well. Assuring
his readers that it would require several lifetimes to make anything approaching an adequate accounting of them, Latourette
nevertheless makes a salutary contribution to our understanding.
I can but touch on it here. I will proceed by referring to a few
examples of "great century advances" and then by underscoring
some post-Enlightenment ideas that Latourette says threaten the
very existence of Christianity.

> In the nineteenth century Christianity spread in associa-
> tion with the expansion of Europe. . . . In the twentieth
> century Western Europe fell into decline. . . . Yet, as revolt
> ended the political and economic empires of Western
> European nations, much which had issued from Western
> Europe was eagerly adopted. Natural sciences, industrial
> processes, mechanical appliances, forms of government,
> kinds of education, and ideologies which had originated
> in Western Europe continued to spread. Here, as in

Western Europe, they worked revolution. Here, as there, they threatened the very existence of Christianity.[1]

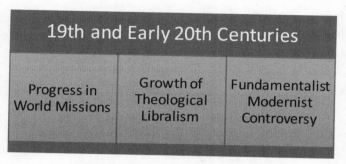

19th and Early 20th Centuries

| Progress in World Missions | Growth of Theological Libralism | Fundamentalist Modernist Controversy |

Figure 5. Great Century and Gathering Storm

"Great Century" Mission Advances

The nineteenth century was a century of progress in world missions the like of which had never been known. Most nineteenth-century advances are well-known to Evangelicals, but I will list some that have become part and parcel of modern missions.

General Agreement on the Applicability of the Great Commission

General doubt as to the applicability of the Great Commission to the church persisted right on through the Reformation and to the end of the "Great Century." Like the Reformers themselves, a significant number of clergy in many communions thought that the Great Commission had been given to the apostles and was fulfilled by them. They saw the church as having no such abiding commission. It took the "Great Century" and the "Great Awakening" to effect change.

---

1. Latourette, *Christianity in a Revolutionary Age*, 1:viii.

Proliferation of Mission Organizations

The organization of numerous of Carey's "means" (i.e., sending agencies or missionary organizations to facilitate and oversee missionary work) tended to be outgrowths of the various denominations. As the century wore on, more and more so-called "faith missions" and missions devoted to such tasks as reaching unreached people groups, Bible translation and distribution, urban evangelization, and ameliorative projects were organized.

Occupation of New Mission Fields

Missionary work was first undertaken in India (Carey) and Burma (Judson), but very soon other areas were added: Samoa and other South Sea islands and Hawaii; Iran, Egypt, Syria, Lebanon, and Turkey in the Middle East; Sierra Leone, Ghana, Nigeria, and South Africa in Africa; China, Japan, and the Philippines in Asia, among others. Missions that occupied coastal lands were later augmented by missions that concentrated on inland areas and populations.

An Increase in the Number of "Supportive" Ministries

Though central to missionary work in the Great Century was the spread of the gospel by preaching, teaching, and Bible translation and distribution, missionaries normally augmented those ministries with humanitarian and social efforts of various kinds. These efforts, however, were generally referred to as "secondary" or "supportive" of the main work of evangelizing and church development.

An Added Number of Women

Often cited as aspects of Great Century missions are the involvement and contributions of women. It has been said that the missionary force came to be constituted of one-third single women, one-third married women, and one-third men.

The Introduction of "Indigenous Church" Strategy

Church-planting and development was central to nineteenth-century missions from the outset, but it was not until the time of Henry Venn (1796–1873) of the Church Missionary Society and Rufus Anderson (1796–1880) of the American Board of Commissioners for Foreign Missions that the term "indigenous" was used to describe the ideal relationship between the church and the receiving culture—namely, that the planted churches should be self-supporting, self-governing, and self-propagating. Other theorists-practitioners such as John L. Nevius (1829–93) and Roland Allen (1869–1947) embellished the theory, but the idea and goal of establishing indigenous churches remained as the stated goal of many evangelical missions well into the twentieth century.

Efforts to Complete World Evangelization

This emphasis became increasingly apparent toward the close of the century as one might expect. In point of fact, the famous Student Volunteer movement for Foreign Missions resulted from an 1886 missions conference in Northfield with the motto "the evangelization of the world in this generation." The 1890s witnessed a national effort to "evangelize the world by the year 1900."

An Eschatological Emphasis on "Bringing Back the King"

Premillennial eschatology in general and the premillennial dispensationalism of J. N. Darby and C. I. Scofield in particular became prominent among Evangelicals in the Bible School movement at the end of the nineteenth century and throughout most of the twentieth. Their eschatology also came to be a prominent factor in missions, especially in the campaign to evangelize the world by the end of the century. It was emphasized that the evangelization of the world would result in "bringing back the King."

Other advances could be mentioned but hopefully those listed above convey something of the dedication and fervor with which "Great Century" mission was undertaken.

The Gathering Storm

Dockery and George follow up their assessment of the Enlightenment with the explanation that the Christian consensus that had existed from the fourth through the sixteenth centuries was invaded by a radical secular spirit. Enlightenment philosophy stressed the primacy of nature and reason over special revelation. Along with its elevation of reason, the Enlightenment reflected "a low view of sin, an anti-supernatural bias, and an ongoing questioning of the place of authority and tradition."[2] In church, school, and mission, theologians loosened and even abandoned doctrinal "tethers" that bound the church to the "stake" of Scripture authority. In place of "what does the Bible say?" many theologians wanted to know "how people *felt*." B. J. Longfield says that liberal scholars in general

> contended that experience and feelings, not creeds or doctrine, provided the foundation of Christianity. The ultimate authority for faith was the self-evidencing testimony of the heart to the individual believer. Liberals insisted that Christianity was a growing and changing life rather than a static creed, ritual or organization. Doctrines, which were nothing more than the tentative and historically limited expressions of abiding religious sentiment, necessarily required periodic reformulation to adjust to the ever-expanding knowledge of mankind. *Modernists thus deplored the continuing division of the church over anachronistic doctrinal disputes and became enthusiastic supporters of efforts for ecclesiastical reunion.*[3]

It is important that we take a brief look at the storm of controversy that nevertheless broke out between modernists and

2. Dockery and George, *Great Tradition*, 47–48.
3. Longfield, "Liberalism/Modernism," 646–48 (emphasis mine).

fundamentalists over doctrinal matters at the end of the nineteenth century and the beginning of the twentieth. Before we do so, however, it may be helpful to survey just a few of the basic ideas advocated by earlier philosopher-theologians—ideas that contributed mightily to that controversy.

Some Influential Philosopher-Theologians of the Eighteenth and Nineteenth Centuries

Mention the beginnings of modern theology and a number of familiar names will soon surface. Four of them may well be Immanuel Kant, Friedrich Schleiermacher, George Hegel, and Albrecht Ritschl—intellectual precursors of modernism.

1. Immanuel Kant (1724–1804). According to Kant, the world of God and the soul is the world of *noumena* as distinguished from the world of *phenomena.* It cannot be known by reason but only by a sense of *social obligation* or *conscience.* There is no place for objective revelation in the Bible. Like every other book, the Bible is subject to historical criticism.

2. Friedrich Schleiermacher (1768–1834). Early on in his career Schleiermacher took a page from Spinoza and, believing that the world itself was perfect and harmonious, tended to identify God with a perfect world. He taught that religion is a natural activity and that, at their best, religious people grasp this God-world system by *intuition.* Religion is an emotional response to that which is intuitively understood.

   Schleiermacher is of special interest to missiologists because of his association with Halle and *Herrnhut.* He was a Reformed Church minister who became Professor of Theology at Halle and, later, the University of Berlin. Schleiermacher and his theology found a home at the University of Halle, which is somewhat ironic but not at all incomprehensible. Already on the eve of the First Great Awakening, the famous Congregational Puritan minister in Boston, Cotton Mather, had written to Francke in Halle (and to missionaries in Tranquebar as well) agreeing that a sense of the nearness of Christ's return enhanced both a spirit of revival and a sense of missionary obligation, but adding, "A world-wide preaching of the eternal Gospel, *free from confessional limitations*, would help to usher in that great outpouring of the Spirit which would be one of the signs of the end of the age"[4].

This illustrates a weakness early on which some Pietists tend to remain susceptible to in the present day—the tendency to downgrade right belief and doctrinal orthodoxy in favor of Bible reading, spiritual experience, and "separated living." It is not unreasonable to conclude that Pietists (and other believers as well) were influenced by Schleiermacher's subjectivism and experientialism as early as the first years of the nineteenth century.

As for the Puritans, when Calvinist leaders at Harvard came under the influence of Unitarian theologians (who also rejected revelation and supernaturalism) there also came to be a general turn in American churches and society away from Pilgrim Christianity, Calvinistic Pietism, and a more traditional understanding of the kingdom of God.

This bit of history shows that creedal and confessional "tethers" can indeed become "dead letters" devoid of the kind of commitment necessary to sustain a meaningful grip on either the "stake" of Scripture or the "cords" of high-flying kites. But it also shows that, without those "tethers," Christian experience easily loses a sense of direction.

3. Georg W. F. Hegel (1770–1831). Hegel taught that the Absolute (i.e., God) manifests himself in history, not in a person or in a book, and he does so by logical resolutions to a series of contradictions. Thesis and antithesis are reconciled into a synthesis which, in turn, becomes the new thesis for which there is an antithesis, and so on and on and on. As strange as this may seem, Hegel's theory of these manifestations of God

4. Neill, *History of Christian Missions*, 203 (emphasis mine).

in history is important because it is basic to Karl Marx and Marxist social theory.

4. Albrecht Ritschl (1822–89). Latest of the four scholars mentioned here, Ritschl's work nevertheless preceded the liberal–fundamentalist debates that took place at the close of the nineteenth century. For Ritschl, a community consciousness of dependence is the foundation of religion. It follows that religion is basically subjective whether one agrees that it is based on community conscience and/or on love as exemplified by the Gospels—neither of which is necessarily supernatural.

Early Radical Textual Critics

In one sense, the Bible is like every other literary work—scholars examine the text in an effort to determine whether or not it is as it was when it came from the mind and hands of the original author (lower criticism). They also examine the historical background of the included books (higher criticism). In another sense, however, the Bible is like no other book. Its human writers wrote under the inspiration of the Holy Spirit so as to make the biblical text both human and divine. That fact makes higher criticism especially vulnerable to the radical ideas of the critics in much the same way as Christian philosophy-theology is vulnerable to the radical ideas of philosophers and theologians.

When, in nineteenth-century Germany, some textual critics combined evolutionary ideas with religious phenomena, the outcome was *radical textual criticism.* Early radical critics of this type were Jean Astruch (1684–1766) and Johann G. Eichhorn (1752–1827), Hermann S. Reimarius 1694–1778), and Gotthold Lessing (1729–81). Later and more immediate to the modernist-fundamentalist debates at the close of the nineteenth century were the theories of Julius Wellhausen (1844–1918) on the authorship of the Pentateuch and Ferdinand C. Bauer (1792–1860) on the chronology and nature of the books of the New Testament.

1. Ferdinand Bauer. In the 1830s Bauer argued that there are major differences in the ways in which New Testament writers and the early church view Judaism, Christ, and the gospel. Peter's writings, for example, understood Judaism as emphasizing the law and the Messiah. Paul's writings emphasized grace rather than law. So there are different approaches, and the critic has to "peel" some of them away in order to get to the kernel of New Testament teaching.

2. The Graf-Wellhausen theory. In the middle of the nineteenth century various liberal scholars proposed that the Pentateuch was the work of two authors, not the work of Moses alone. Graf and Wellhausen went even further by suggesting that the Pentateuch was the work of *four* authors in addition to Moses. This, of course, had the effect of making the Pentateuch mainly the work of human authors and allowed them to be treated accordingly.

Other Contributors to the "Storm"

1. Horace Bushnell (1802–76) and *"Christian Nurture."* Bushnell proposed a "new habit of thought" (termed "Christian nurture") that ran contrary to revival, conversion, miracles, and formal Christian doctrine. Children should be brought up as Christians not knowing anything else. Doctrine should be "formulated Christian experience."

2. Charles Darwin (1809–82) and his *On the Origin of Species* (1859). When dealing with the theological consequences of what he terms the "intellectual revolution" of this period, Union Theological Seminary's church historian Robert T. Handy maintains that the nineteenth-century division in Protestantism was primarily due to the influence of Charles Darwin and his book *On the Origin of Species* (1859). Handy says that in the earlier part of the nineteenth century, the churches had found ways of dealing with the challenges of rationalism, romanticism, and *idealism because at that time the authority*

of the Bible was generally assumed. But in the later part of the century this was destined to change due in large part, as Handy sees it, to the work of Darwin. Handy writes,

> Then came the impact of Charles Darwin's *Origin of Species* (1859). His extensive research gave the theory of evolution plausibility and clarity, while his later writings more directly challenged traditional views of human origins. Intense debates ensued, and a rift opened between those who accepted evolution in some form and those who rejected it. Evolutionary thought also encouraged critical approaches to historical and literary study, which had an impact on the study of the Bible. The arguments in the churches over evolution had been sharp enough; those that emerged a decade or two later over the critical study of the Bible were even fiercer. Many Christians found that the historical approach to the Bible—viewing it as a collection of writings gathered over a long period of time—was liberating, allowing them to separate its spiritual message from an outworn cosmology. Others found this method an impious mistreatment of the divine and authoritative Word of God. The controversies divided the churches into opposing camps which have been in tension ever since. Some felt themselves obliged to choose between science and religion, while others found ways to mediate between the two.[5]

3. Walter Rauschenbusch (1861–1918) and the Social Gospel. The term "Social Gospel" was popularized in the late nineteenth century, but the idea that the mission of Christians is to promote the welfare of workers more than—or even rather than—the salvation of individuals has a long history. In the middle of the nineteenth century it was promoted by William Ellery Channing, Horace Bushnell, Theodore Parker, Washington Gladden, and especially by the theologian of the movement, Walter Rauschenbusch. Rauschenbusch, in

5. Handy, *History of the Churches*, 264–65.

effect, identified Jesus's view of the kingdom with the out-come of Darwin's evolutionary hypothesis and the gospel as the present achievement of peace and prosperity. He died a heartbroken man when in the First World War he witnessed his "Christian" native Germany at war with his "Christian" adopted America. His Social Gospel itself awaited popularity at a later time and in different formulations.

The Storm Breaks:
The Fundamentalist–Modernist Controversy

So much history led up to—and so much history led out from—the so-called fundamentalist–modernist controversy at the turn of the nineteenth and twentieth centuries that it is extremely dif-ficult to summarize both coherently and concisely. At any rate, it took place when the pent-up forces of the Enlightenment and the philosophical-theological factors we have been considering came to bear upon the more fundamental and orthodox theology of conservatives in general and fundamentalists in particular. Cer-tain questions basic to the great tradition of Christian thinking were at its core.

The Fundamentals: True or False?

A sermon by A. C. Dixon in 1909 led Lyman and Milton Stewart to donate a sizeable amount of money to the preparation, publica-tion, and distribution of a twelve-volume set of books entitled *The Fundamentals: A Testimony to Truth* (1910–15). The work was de-signed to counter the liberalism–modernism that by then prevailed in many denominations. Scholars from both Europe and America including men like M. G. Kyle, James Orr, B. B. Warfield, and R. A. Torrey contributed chapters in which most of them defended the inerrancy and authority of Scripture as over against the experien-tial grounding of liberalism. They and other scholars also wrote on major doctrinal themes such as the Trinity of the Godhead, virgin birth, and deity of Christ, miracles, the substitutionary atonement, bodily resurrection, salvation by grace through faith, and still others. These writings were by no means simple treatises but, rather, robust and engaging tomes well calculated to challenge the conclusions of the most erudite of liberal theologians and higher critics. Due to the generosity of the Stewarts, three million sets were sent out gratis to Protestant religious workers worldwide! That alone was sufficient to ensure the importance of the debate and the significance of its outcome.

Scripture: Human or Divine?

Charles Hodge (1797–1878) and his student and successor at Princeton, B. B. Warfield (1851–1921), were among the many who challenged the naturalistic theories of liberal theologians and higher critics that we have considered and others as well. After teaching biblical literature for four years at Princeton Seminary, Hodge went to Europe to study much of the philosophy and theology to which we have just referred from 1826 to 1828. He then returned to Princeton where he taught until 1878. During that time he became known as one of America's most respected Presbyterian theologians.

Warfield succeeded Hodge as professor of didactic and polemic theology at Princeton and, in that capacity and as editor of *The Princeton Review*, authored numerous scholarly works. Together with Hodge he upheld Augustine, Calvin, and Reformed confessions and opposed the subjectivity of Schleiermacher and liberals in general. Together with Charles Hodge's son, A. A. Hodge, Warfield coauthored the 1881 monograph *Inspiration* in which they upheld Bible inspiration as verbal plenary and the Bible itself to be totally trustworthy and without error.

Evolution: Acceptable or Unacceptable?

On the wider civic scene as well as within the church and its institutions, Darwin's biological evolution precipitated one of the most divisive and bitter debates of modern history. *On the Origin of Species* (1859) challenged special creation and therefore the authority of Scripture—a debate that sharpened and became increasingly bitter in the 1870s. In 1925 opposition to the teaching of evolution in public schools resulted in the famous "monkey trial" of teacher John Scopes in Dayton, Tennessee. Scopes—on trial for teaching evolution—was prosecuted by William Jennings Bryan and defended by Clarence Darrow. Scopes lost. But, like other challenges to doctrinal orthodoxy and Scripture authority, the debate has been intense and has continued to the present day—indeed, to the present hour—not only in Europe and the Americas but in Asia and Africa as well.

Closing Reflections

What I have been calling the "storm" gathered in the nineteenth century, broke toward the turn of the twentieth, and blew across Europe and America and many places around the world. In ways that are only partly explicable in a few paragraphs, I experienced the winds of that storm if only on its fringes. My paternal grandfather was a prominent Unitarian and Universalist. I was born into a Methodist church where sermons were based on secular classics as much or more than the Bible. In my youth I regularly attended a Pentecostal church. As an undergraduate student I was privileged to study philosophy under a world-class faculty—not one of whom seemed to agree with any other. (The most agnostic and antagonistic among them was the daughter of a Protestant pastor.) One of the most popular was a Kierkegaardian existentialist, later to become dean of Yale Divinity School.

From 1957 to 1962 I had the unique privilege of ministering in the shadow of Doshisha University in Kyoto, Japan. Doshisha is a Congregationalist university long since given to the liberalism of the late nineteenth century. That story, in fact, is most appropriate here so I will deviate from my usual form in order to relate it.

In the 1880s Doshisha had been the home of a great revival. Classes were suspended for weeks while students and faculty gave themselves to prayer and witness. Before the revival came to an end, two hundred students had been baptized. But then two German missionaries of the Evangelical Protestant Mission, Wilfred Spinner and Otto Schmiedel, brought higher criticism to Japan direct from Germany. Shortly after, Unitarianism and universalism arrived from America. The faith of many Japanese Christian leaders was shaken. A well-known scholar, Danjo Ebina, came to the conclusion that the Jehovah of the Bible and the Great Center of Heaven God of the Kojiki were one and the same. The well-known Kanzo Uchimura taught that Christ is the Sun but Buddha is the Moon. Anyone who loves the Sun will love the Moon also. Paul Kanamori gave up on the gospel, turned from Christian ministry, but later repented and became one of Japan's greatest evangelists.

Caught in the maelstrom of religious thinking such as this, the revival ceased and not a few Doshisha faculty members defected from the faith. As we discovered, the younger churches have different needs. Theological storms sometimes leapfrog from place to place and church to church. The teaching task may be enormous; "all he commanded" may be inclusive of more of the "great tradition of Christian thinking" than we first thought! Missionaries have every reason to thank linguists, cultural anthropologists, and cross-culturalists. It is important to know and understand *culture*, but it is even more important to know and understand Christian theology and thinking—*the Christ and gospel of the fathers, the Reformers, and the Revivalists!*

Chapter 5

The Aftermath of the Storm, Part One

Twentieth-Century Conciliarism and Ecumenism

INCIPIENT IN THE DIVISIONS in the eighteenth and nineteenth centuries were the ecclesiastical and theological developments of the twentieth, both the more fundamental/evangelical and the more liberal/conciliar. We will deal with the former in ensuing chapters, but it is important that we first give attention to liberal/conciliar ecclesiastical and missiological developments—important not just as history but also as a comparison of the workings and outcomes of two very different ways of dealing with the word and work of God.

At both national and international levels, liberal/conciliar movements grew out of the Evangelical Alliance established in London in 1846 and reorganized in 1867. That organization provided the foundation for ecumenical organizations and activities in the United States and later—primarily through a world missions conference in Edinburgh in 1910—the World Council of Churches.

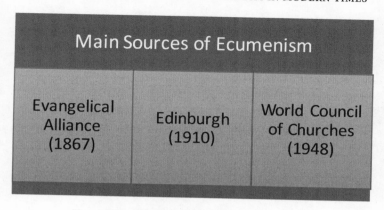

Figure 6. Twentieth-century conciliarism/ecumenism

The Mainline Denominations
and the Conciliar Movement

The main ecumenical organizations in the United States were the Federal Council of Churches of Christ in America (FCCC, 1908) and, later on, the National Council of Churches of Christ (NCCC, 1950) composed of thirty-three denominations and twelve interdenominational agencies. According to P. A. Crow, the National Council of Churches of Christ sought to "bring the implications of the gospel to the life and problems of church and society" through a wide variety of enterprises having to do with the establishment of world peace; opposing racism in the United States and South Africa; developing relationships with Christians in Vietnam and the Eastern Bloc as well as relief, development, evangelism, and Bible translation.[1] At one point, some 85 percent of the total budget of the National Council went to the relief programs of the Church World Service!

At first the NCCC grew rather significantly, but as it entered the 1980s it began to experience more difficult times. Originally it had expressed itself as based on "Jesus Christ as divine Lord and Savior." But in 1981 it restructured its work and redefined itself.

---

1. Crow, "National Council of Churches," 798–99.

Instead of "a cooperative agency of the churches" it became "a community of Christian communions which, in response to the gospel revealed in the Scriptures, confess Jesus Christ, the incarnate Word of God as Savior and Lord." If the change was designed to attract more Christian denominations, organizations, and individuals to the council, the change was not a success. It largely became a service agency.[2] By the late 1980s contributions were down 50 percent from 1975, and its staff had been cut from 187 two decades before to sixty-one.[3]

The "Fatal Flaw" at Edinburgh 1910

Writing in 1954 Earle Cairns felt justified in saying,

> Not since the days of the ecumenical councils at Nicaea, Constantinople, and Chalcedon in the fourth and fifth centuries has there been such a wave of cooperation among churches as there has been in recent years. Founded in London in 1846, with nearly eight hundred present, the Evangelical Alliance had a definite theological statement that linked individuals rather than churches. Consequently, the alliance became inactive about 1900 as other organizations to promote interdenominational and international cooperation came into being. But it marked the first step in the development of a modern ecumenical body.[4]

By far the most prominent "other organization" proved to be the World Council of Churches (WCC) that grew out of the famed World Conference on Missions held in Edinburgh, Scotland, in 1910. In order to assure harmony and unity at Edinburgh, John Mott and fellow organizers such as Charles Brent, Nathan Soderblom, and William Temple decided that the program would provide no opportunity for discussion of Christian

2. Crow, "National Council of Churches," 798–99.
3. Crow, "National Council of Churches," 798–99.
4. Cairns, *Christianity through the Centuries*, 467.

doctrine or controversial questions.[5] That decision resulted in what John Stott termed a "fatal flaw" and what I have termed "the Edinburgh Error."[6] Stott writes:

> Theologically, the fatal flaw at Edinburgh was not so much doctrinal disagreement as apparent doctrinal indifference, since doctrine was not on the agenda. Vital themes like the content of the gospel, the theology of evangelism and the nature of the church were not discussed. The reason is that Randall Davidson, Archbishop of Canterbury, as a condition of participation at Edinburgh, secured a promise from John R. Mott that doctrinal debate could be excluded. *In consequence, the theological challenges of the day were not faced. And, during the decades that followed, the poison of theological liberalism seeped into the bloodstream of western universities and seminaries, and largely immobilized the churches' mission.*[7]

The "Fatal Flaw" and Its Reverberations in the World Council of Churches

The story is familiar to students of twentieth-century missions/missiology. Out of Edinburgh 1910 flowed not one but three interchurch organizations: the International Missionary Council (IMC, 1921), the Conference on Life and Work (1925), and the Conference on Faith and Order (1927). Arthur Johnston writes:

> Inspired by the social gospel, [Life and Work] assumed responsibility for some of the areas of social work anticipated by the IMC. . . . [Faith and Order] spoke of unity as necessary for the missionary enterprise of the Church. Increased attention was given to the authority of an

5. Mott had just experienced some memorable interdenominational and intermission conferences among missionaries in Asia that purposely downplayed doctrinal and ecclesiastical divisions. Ralph Winter once told me that Mott deeply desired the same outcome at Edinburgh and therefore proposed the probation of such discussions.

6. Hesselgrave, "Correct the Edinburgh Error?," 121–49.

7. Stott, "Historical Introduction," xii (emphasis mine).

organized united Church and its responsibility for evangelism. It was decided that the studies of Faith and Order should become the unofficial IMC theological position.[8]

Subsequently, Life and Work and Faith and Order together formed the World Council of Churches (WCC) in Amsterdam in 1948. Upon its formation, the faith statement of the WCC consisted of but one affirmation: "The World Council of Churches is a fellowship of churches which confess the Lord Jesus Christ as Lord and Savior." At the insistence of the Eastern Orthodox Church the words "according to the Scriptures and therefore seek to fulfill together their common calling to the glory of the one God—Father, Son and Holy Spirit" were added at New Delhi in 1961. Also at New Delhi, the IMC was integrated into the WCC as its Division of World Mission and Evangelism (DWME) against the wishes of some of its most prominent members. They felt that the move would work to the disadvantage of missions.

They proved to be right. In another generation ecumenists had come full circle. Out of Edinburgh they had succeeded in evolving an ecumenical movement dedicated to changing the world but largely devoid of both the biblical faith and spiritual energy required to accomplish that task. By the time they met in Uppsala in 1968, they had been so impacted by sub-orthodox theology, social studies, and a secular worldview that they were better prepared to follow a byline of the conference and "Let the world set the agenda."

The Consequences of a "Tetherless Unity"
in the Ecumenical Movement

In 1932, a Laymen's Foreign Missionary Committee under the leadership of Harvard's William E. Hocking reported that, in the future, missions should emphasize social efforts, education, and medicine, not evangelism.[9] Hendrik Kraemer took issue, but the

8. Johnston, *Battle for World Evangelism*, 58–59.

9. Hocking, *Re-thinking Missions*, 83.

die was cast. James Scherer suggests that, after the Second World War, ecumenists placed their stamp of approval on a church-centered view of missions that replaced the earlier personal conversion view.[10] By the mid-1960s, R. Pierce Beaver exclaimed, "Service or relief programs, so closely associated with interchurch aid *are* mission."[11] Finally, at more or less the same time, George Vicedom was popularizing *Missio Dei* ("mission of God") that was variously interpreted but basically held that missions were first and foremost the mission of God and only secondarily the mission of the church. *Missio Dei* had the effect of changing the focus of missions from the Great Commission as such to the work of God in building his kingdom.

Well before the Uppsala, Sweden, conference in 1968 Donald McGavran attempted to persuade the WCC to reverse course by including a serious discussion on the dire need to reach the unevangelized with the gospel in the official program. In a variety of venues McGavran urged Uppsala organizers to remember the "2 billion unevangelized."[12] Organizers paid little or no heed. The theme they chose was "Behold I make all things new" and, as noted above, "Let the world set the agenda." Uppsala did not eliminate discussions on the nature and meaning of mission in subsequent gatherings, but the Uppsala gathering was a harbinger of the fate of twentieth-century ecumenical missions. The conciliar mainline denominations that had supplied 80 percent of the Protestant missionary force in the early years of the twentieth century supplied only 6 percent of it at the close of the century.[13]

Closing Reflections

Sponsored by the World Council of Churches, the centennial in Edinburgh from June 2 to 6, 2010 brought some three hundred

10. Scherer, "Church, Kingdom, and Missio Dei," 83.

11. Beaver, *From Missions to Mission*, 110 (emphasis in original).

12. Hesselgrave, *Paradigms in Conflict*, 325; see also 317–26.

13. Moreau, "Putting the Survey in Perspective," 4, 34.

conferees from sixty nations. According to WCC General Secretary Olav Fykse Tveit, its purpose was "to launch together a new beginning for common mission in the 21st century."[14] Reinforcing the ecumenical concern for unity, "Tveit also highlighted that mission and unity are inseparable: 'Mission and unity belong together. To be one in Christ is to witness together to Christ.'"[15] Emphasizing the need for contemporary Christian missions to reconcile evangelization and prophetic witness, Tveit went on to tell conferees that "to witness to Christ is both evangelism and the prophetic stand for Christ's will for justice, peace, and care of creation."[16]

Certain observations certainly seem justified.

- First, study documents make it clear that mission is no longer based on the Bible alone but on *three* bases: *experience or context, diverse understandings of the biblical text, and new theological frameworks.*

- Second, the initial draft of the Common Call issued by the conference forwards the notion that "God's mission" (*missio Dei*) is especially concerned with liberation and justice. Only later was the word "evangelism" inserted![17]

- Third, the 2010 Edinburgh Conference celebrated not only a diversity of ethnicities, cultures, and experiences but also *a diversity of understandings of Scripture authority, diverse understandings of the content of the gospel, and diverse understandings of the meaning of mission—in fact, diverse understandings of the very nature of God and the uniqueness of Christ.*

In short, by 2010 the World Council of Churches had become but a shadow of its former self. It had neither the kind of faith nor the kind of support that bespoke future success.

---

14. Kirsteen and Anderson, "Mission Today and Tomorrow," 9.

15. "World Mission Conference Begins in Edinburgh."

16. Kirsteen and Anderson, "Mission Today and Tomorrow", 9.

17. Fox, "Account of Edinburgh 2010," 88–93, 89.

Chapter 6

The Aftermath of the Storm, Part Two

Twentieth-Century Fundamentalism
and Evangelicalism

THE EARLY TWENTIETH CENTURY also witnessed the beginnings of fundamentalist and, somewhat later, evangelical organizations and cooperative ministries that changed the face of Protestant Christianity mightily and permanently. According to Joel Carpenter, for example, the gap in our knowledge of the contribution of the fundamentalist movement to world missions is a "critical missing piece"[1] in American and global religious history. To quote Carpenter,

> The fundamentalists . . . contributed about one out of every seven North American Protestant missionaries in the mid-1930s, and by the early 1950s, the fundamentalists' portion had doubled. Their dynamic missionary movement was an important factor, along with other evangelical missions efforts, in the survival and growth of the foreign missions enterprise in the twentieth century.[2]

1. Carpenter, "Propagating the Faith," 93.
2. Carpenter, "Propagating the Faith," 92–132, especially 93.

But, of course, that was just the beginning. It does not take into account the evangelical organizations and efforts that began with the formation of the National Association of Evangelicals beginning in 1943–44. Less than thirty years later, in 1970, Ralph Winter could write about the twenty-five years from 1945 to 1969 as being the "unbelievable years" in missions, not solely but largely because of the growth and exploits of evangelical missions after the close of World War II.[3] It's a story that deserves to be told and retold. But it is not entirely positive and hopeful. It has another side and that side also must be told.

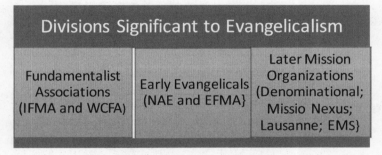

Divisions Significant to Evangelicalism

Fundamentalist Associations (IFMA and WCFA)	Early Evangelicals (NAE and EFMA}	Later Mission Organizations (Denominational; Missio Nexus; Lausanne; EMS}

Figure 7. Twentieth-century fundamentalism and Evangelicalism

When Evangelicals found themselves at odds with fundamentalists over their divisiveness and lack of social concern, Evangelicals formed their own organizations. Once organized, however, Evangelicals themselves experienced divisions of various kinds and often disagreed as to the kind and place of social involvement in the mission of the church. That record is well known to "insiders" but not so well known to believers outside evangelical schools and the headquarters and conferences of the missions themselves. That is the story that will be emphasized in the following pages—not because of its controversial nature but because of its incontrovertible importance. As a matter of fact, differences among Evangelicals have been of such a nature that some theologians and missiologists are genuinely concerned for

3. Winter, *Twenty-Five Unbelievable Years.*

the future of the movement. It is imperative, then, that committed Evangelicals generally know why.

Early Fundamentalism: The Interdenominational Foreign Mission Association and the World Christian Fundamentals Association

It has been maintained that the action of "faith mission" leaders in forming the Interdenominational Foreign Mission Association of North America (IFMA) was in response to a perceived denominational elitism at Edinburgh. Be that as it may, it was not until September 1917 that "faith mission" leaders scheduled a meeting in Princeton, New Jersey. Chaired by Henry W. Frost, leaders of the Africa Inland Mission, China Inland Mission, Sudan Interior Mission, and several other missions organized the Interdenominational Foreign Mission Association of North America (IFMA, more recently CrossGlobal Link and now part of Missio Nexus).

While Edinburgh left matters of doctrine and discipline to represented (largely mainline conciliar) denominations, one of the first items of business for the fundamentalists was to draw up a preliminary *Doctrinal Basis* of some cardinal doctrines of the Christian faith as a basis of fellowship and cooperation.[4] Building on the work of conservative scholars who had collaborated in producing *The Fundamentals: A Testimony to the Truth*, leaders identified eight such doctrines beginning with the verbal inspiration and the inerrant authority of Scripture and including statements on the Trinity, the fall, the deity of Christ, salvation by faith, the imminent and personal return of Christ, heaven and hell, the church, and Christian mission.[5]

Two years later, in 1919, the World Christian Fundamentals Association (WCFA) was also formed under the leadership of William B. Riley. It was active in sponsoring meetings and writings

---

4. Frizen, *75 Years of IFMA*, 119–20.

5. Frizen, *75 Years of IFMA*, 109–10; see also 435–36.

on behalf of the fundamentalist cause for a number of years but existed as a separate organization for little more than thirty years.

Early Evangelicals: The National Association of Evangelicals and the Evangelical Fellowship of Mission Agencies

During the middle 1940s theologically conservative leaders such as J. Elwin Wright, Harold J. Ockenga, Carl F. H. Henry, and Billy Graham took the lead in bringing Evangelicals together. Finding themselves at odds especially with liberals on the left but also with fundamentalism and its "denominational separatism and intellectual and cultural isolationism"[6] on the right, leaders formed the National Association of Evangelicals (NAE) in 1943. An NAE affiliate, the Evangelical Fellowship of Mission Agencies (EFMA) was formed in 1945 with direction from Clyde Taylor.

As we have noted, the year 1945 signaled the beginning of Winter's "twenty-five unbelievable years."[7] After 1945 tens of thousands of American GIs came home from their encounters with faraway lands and peoples only to prepare to return to those same lands and peoples with the gospel. The period witnessed the missionary commitment of the Auca martyrs; saw the rapid growth of student movements such as InterVarsity Christian Fellowship, Campus Crusade for Christ, and the Navigators; featured the Billy Graham evangelistic crusades; gave birth to new mission emphases in Bible colleges such as Columbia, Nyack, and Moody and in seminaries such as Fuller, Gordon-Conwell, and Trinity; provided a locus for various missions and enterprises at the US Center for World Mission in Pasadena; and gave rise to Evangelism-in-Depth, Evangelism Explosion, Theological Education by Extension, and Church Growth. In the United States, 1976 was declared to be the "Year of the Evangelical" and with good reason.[8] And this was just the beginning. If we also consider

---

6. McGee, "Evangelical Movement," 338.

7. Winter, *Twenty-Five Unbelievable Years*, 3.

8. Kucharsky, "Year of the Evangelical," 12.

evangelical advances of the years that remained to the twentieth century, they are nothing short of staggering. Literally hundreds of missionary organizations, movements, and ministries of all kinds emerged—most of them "staked" in some way in Scripture and "tethered" in some fashion to a biblical gospel.

At first, leaders of this new movement were sometimes called "*neo*" or "new" Evangelicals and the movement itself "*neo*" or "new" Evangelicalism, but by the 1960s they and their movement had become part of the conservative mainstream. From that time the word "new" has usually been dropped and the words "Evangelicals" and "Evangelicalism" have served to identify the larger movement. As Wade Coggins put it,

> The EFMA broke new ground by pulling together evangelicals from various traditions, ranging from Baptist to Reformed, Mennonite, Holiness and Pentecostal. As a variety of evangelical denominations, missions and service agencies, and student ministries joined the association, the EFMA experienced rapid growth.[9]

It is worth noting in passing that, in the same context, Coggins makes reference to the EFMA's "solid commitment on the evangelical theological essentials" and its mention of "agencies that conform to specific doctrinal and financial standards."[10] Given the organization's ecclesiastical inclusivism, however, questions that were at least apparent at that time have become more apparent now. And those questions merit exploration.

"Windows" on the Evangelical Movement: Four Representative Organizations

The evangelical movement of the last three-quarters of a century is inclusive of so many different churches, so many diverse organizations, so many distinctive programs that it is extremely difficult to make generalizations that define and describe the whole of it. I

9. Coggins, "Evangelical Fellowship," 332.
10. Coggins, "Evangelical Fellowship," 332.

prefer rather to deal with four evangelical (largely) major organizations that can be considered more or less representative of the movement and therefore serve as "windows" on some of its major characteristics. In doing so, I recognize that leaders of the various organizations may take exception to aspects of my characterizations and some of the implications I draw from them.

A "Denominational" Mission: The International Mission Board (IMB) of the Southern Baptist Convention

In 1845 southern Baptists split from northern Baptists over issues having to do with slavery and missions. Their mission arm (then called the Foreign Mission Board) barely survived the War and Restoration period but expanded its ministry in the twentieth century to the degree that the IMB now constitutes one of the largest and most influential Protestant denominational missionary forces in the world.

The Southern Baptist Convention (SBC) and its constituent parts are unique. The SBC does not consider itself to be a "denomination" as such, though it operates much as many Free Church denominations do in that local churches are free to govern themselves within certain basic parameters. The SBC claims no creedal statement, but it does have a confessional statement called the Baptist Faith and Message (there have been four versions: 1925, 1963, 1998, and 2000) that is considered to be a "guide," though not binding except when it is affirmed by the convention meeting in full session.

Southern Baptists are especially important to evangelical missions and the evangelical movement as a whole for a variety of reasons. For one thing, over many years the Southern Baptist Convention has experienced a struggle between "moderates" and "conservatives." (In more recent years there has been a resurgence of conservatism that is almost unprecedented among Protestant denominations in America.) The story of that struggle is instructive. It is told in great detail in James C. Hefley's *The Conservative*

Resurgence in the Southern Baptist Convention[11]—a book that is touted to be the "wrap-up book of *The Truth in Crisis* series and covers seventy years of eventful Southern Baptist history, climaxing in the most revolutionary change of a denomination in American Church history."[12] Whatever else might be said about that "revolutionary change," it should be said that it is not necessarily permanent. Until Christ returns, every generation of Southern Baptists will be asking and answering the same questions, framing and facing the same proposals, and discussing and deciding the same issues. That much is quite sure; the outcomes are not.

Secondly, the International Mission Board of the Southern Baptist Church has much to offer global evangelical missions. Not only is it one of the largest of contemporary missions, its missionary force ranks high in terms of overall qualifications, specialized training, and regular support. Southern Baptist seminaries rank high with well-qualified faculties and more than adequate facilities and library resources. Missionary volunteers have unusual opportunities for guided experience on the various fields prior to their appointment as permanent workers. Recruits are supported by the IMB and not faced with the responsibility of raising their own support.

That said, and in my view, Southern Baptist missions do have tendencies that betray certain weaknesses. They are adversely affected by the theological controversies that afflict the denomination as a whole. And Southern Baptist missions as a whole seem to be on an incessant search for a key strategy or strategies that will render the mission of the church easier and its objectives more readily achievable. At the same time it must be said that this latter characteristic also tends to pertain to evangelical missions generally.

---

11. Hefley, *Conservative Resurgence.*
12. Hefley, *Conservative Resurgence*, back cover.

An Inter-Mission Organization: Missio Nexus

The theme of an October 2011 conference in Scottsdale, Arizona, was "Reset: Mission in a Context of Deep Change." Delegated leaders of CrossGlobal Link (aka IFMA) and the Mission Exchange (aka EFMA) voted to merge their two organizations into one organization called "Missio Nexus." The stated objective was "to develop a *Missio Nexus* for the largest and most inclusive expression of Great Commission–oriented evangelicals in North America that fosters *shared learning, opens doors for collaborative action and produces increased effectiveness.*"[13]

With that objective in mind, leaders melded the faith statements of the two organizations into a new Missio Nexus statement of faith.[14] The new statement of faith omits references to the Bible as "consisting of Old and New Testaments only," as "verbally inspired by the Holy Spirit," and as "inerrant in the original manuscripts"—all of which had been included in the older CrossGlobal Link confession of faith. In place of these phrases they chose the Mission Exchange statement *"We believe the Bible to be the inspired, the only infallible, authoritative Word of God,"* thereby leaving open certain questions having to do with the nature of inspiration and the meaning of "infallible" in this particular context.

As we have seen, CrossGlobal Link (also known as IFMA) and the Mission Exchange (also known as EFMA) had long histories stretching back to the beginnings of fundamentalism and Evangelicalism in America. We have overviewed that history and will have more to say about it in ensuing chapters. Missio Nexus has a short history. To say more than to call attention to the obvious may be premature. The strength of Missio Nexus lies in the fact that it is mainly composed of delegated representatives of evangelical churches and missions and therefore fully capable of making binding and lasting decisions. Its weakness lies in the fact that in its desire to embrace and represent larger and larger segments of the Protestant population Missio Nexus will almost

---

13. See "Who We Are."

14. See "Statement of Faith."

surely come under increased pressure to relinquish traditional conservative aspects of evangelical faith and practice. That being the case, chapters remaining to this book may be of special significance to Missio Nexus and its constituent parts.

An Evangelization Movement: The Lausanne Committee for World Evangelization (LCWE)

The Lausanne movement as such dates back to a World Congress on Evangelism held in Berlin in 1966 and to Billy Graham's burden to bring worldwide clarity and agreement to the subject of evangelism. The Congress on World Evangelization held in Lausanne, Switzerland, in July 1974 and the Lausanne Committee for World Evangelization (LCWE) both grew out of that 1966 Congress on Evangelism but with the concept "world evangelization" having been substituted for the word "evangelism."

It is no stretch to say that the 1974 congress and its "Lausanne Covenant" constitute a most significant chapter in the history of modern evangelical missions. The covenant along with its architect John Stott's follow-up book, *Christian Mission in the Modern World*,[15] refashioned the mission of the church for many Evangelicals, making gospel proclamation and sociopolitical action into "partners" in Christian mission. Stott himself summed up the church's mission as being "everything the church is sent into the world to do."[16]

A vast majority of Lausanne participants—some 2,200 of them—signed the covenant. That number may have been somewhat deceiving, however, because a decade later in 1982 a Lausanne-sponsored Consultation on the Relationship between Evangelism and Social Responsibility (CRESR) held in Grand Rapids, Michigan, was indecisive on the issue. A. Scott Moreau sums it up nicely: "While all agreed that our Christian responsibilities include engagement in meeting social responsibilities, the

15. Stott, *Christian Mission*.
16. Stott, *Christian Mission* 30.

question as to whether this is integral to mission was not resolved to everyone's satisfaction."[17]

A decade and a half after Lausanne I, Lausanne II convened in Manila. It produced the Manila Manifesto, which was considerably longer than the Lausanne Covenant. The manifesto states,

> Our covenant at Lausanne was "to pray, to plan, to work together for the evangelization of the whole world." Our manifesto at Manila is that the whole church is called to take the whole gospel to the whole world, proclaiming Christ until he comes, with all necessary urgency, unity, and sacrifice.

Finally, one hundred years after Edinburgh, in 2010 some four thousand participants from 198 countries met in Cape Town, South Africa, for Lausanne III. Lausanne III produced a most interesting and unusual document. The heading of Part I includes the phrase, "the Cape Town Confession of Faith," but that is preceded by the words, "For the Lord we love" and succeeded by ten extended statements of *beliefs*, yes, but mainly *behaviors that flow from "loves."* Overall the commitment represents a shift from confessional objectivity to experiential subjectivity and as a consequence loses clarity and a clear focus.

Though Trinity Evangelical Divinity School's dean emeritus, Tite Tiénou, holds the Lausanne Covenant especially in high esteem, when writing about it he rightly calls attention to the limitations of documents engendered by conferences and gatherings of the Lausanne variety. He says,

> I think that the challenge for evangelicals is that every one of the Lausanne Congresses was actually an *ad hoc* event. It was organized for the occasion. As a result, continuity between the three is really difficult. Whereas the World Council of Churches or the Roman Catholic Church has an infrastructure behind it, so they have continuity. When evangelicals gather, the people who come are the ones to cause the change when they go home. . . .

17. Moreau, "Consultation of the Relationship," 224.

> They're not answerable to anyone. We came as individuals, not as delegates of our respective churches.[18]

It should be noted that the original text of section eight of the Cape Town Commitment has been augmented to include statements on inerrancy ("In faith we hold the Bible to be inerrant in the original writings, God-breathed, and the complete and final authority for faith and practice") and proclamational mission ("the obligation of all believers, by word and life, to testify to the truth of God's Word"). That is important but it must be remembered that all that Lausanne says and does—and it says and does much—is ad hoc "*for the participants and for the occasion.*"

An Academic Society: The Evangelical Missiological Society (EMS)

The EMS was organized at the instigation and with the support of Donald A. McGavran. The circuitous path which led McGavran from his ecumenical inclinations and associations in the 1920s and 1930s to his emergence as the "Father of Church Growth" in the years following World War II and, finally, to his convinced conservatism of the late 1980s is well worth telling. In this context, however, I will simply refer to a 1988 conversation in which he said in effect,

> David, it is quite pointless to have an academic association in which professors of mission come together to discuss our mission to the world when many of those present do not even believe that men and women are lost. We need a new association all the members of which are in agreement on the basics of orthodox Christian faith.

That conversation resulted in the formation of the EMS and its requirement that all members express agreement with the faith statement(s) of either the IFMA or the EFMA or both. And that, in turn, facilitated not only the publication of numerous papers and pieces important to evangelical mission beliefs and

18. Moll, "Global Reconciliation," 13.

strategies, but also to open examination and evaluation of some of the most important of them. Unfortunately, EMS leaders were not involved when Missio Nexus and its new statement of faith came into being, so, almost overnight, the EMS was bereft of a statement of faith as such.

As this is being written, the EMS identifies its doctrinal orientation as being that of the Lausanne Covenant (not the Lausanne statement of faith referred to above but just the covenant). The covenant is an ad hoc statement at best and hardly the most robust of faith statements, especially for academics of the stature of members of the EMS. The society possesses significant potential for generating new and innovative proposals. In fact, a fairly recent annual meeting of the north-central district of the EMS featured the presentation of almost fifty papers in less than two days! At the same time, the Society has the capacity to conduct open examination and evaluation of cutting-edge proposals such as those that will be referred to in chapters to follow. In my view, given the unique qualifications of its membership, the strength of the EMS lies in its willingness and capability to vet and evaluate proposals that have the highest potential—whether good or bad—for the future of the larger evangelical movement. Its weakness lies in a perceived reluctance on the part of some to do so.

Closing Reflections

Professor of church history at the Assemblies of God Theological Seminary Gary B. McGee addresses the diversity that characterizes the evangelical movement and the issues to which that gives rise. He writes,

> Modern evangelicalism now encompasses an almost unbridgeable diversity of Christians, all loyal to the gospel message, but with varying theological and spiritual orientations. Major groupings consist of Lutherans, Presbyterians, Anglicans, Pentecostals, Baptists, Wesleyans, Mennonites, Brethren, Churches of Christ, and others in the Restoration Movement. To these can be

added Messianic Jews, nondenominational Christians, and constituents of parachurch agencies (e.g., Campus Crusade for Christ). Although controversial, some observers have listed Seventh-Day Adventists; and "Jesus Name" or Oneness Pentecostals belong [sic].[19]

"Almost unbridgeable" but not quite. Evangelicals have maintained some modicum of agreement and cooperation despite their diversity and differences. But evangelicals of today and tomorrow will face global conditions and theological/missiological considerations that await a more united and specific evangelical response than has been the case heretofore. Any way you look at it, this is not 1976. This is not the "Year of the Evangelical." Nor is there much hope that it yet will be. When you hear really good news about Evangelicals, it is almost invariably about some very limited or local situation, or else it is about evangelical advance in the global church. The decline of Christianity in America has been most alarming and has occurred among Evangelicals as well as conciliars in the mainline Protestant denominations. In 1988 white Evangelicals comprised 22 percent of the population. In 2016 that percentage had dwindled to 18 percent. White millennials are less than half as likely to be Christian than were their predecessors a generation ago—fewer than three in ten today as compared to nearly seven in ten of their counterparts a generation ago.[20] *The evangelical part of that history, as briefly summarized above, will be illustrated in chapters yet to come.*

19. McGee, "Evangelical Movement," 338.
20. These statistics come from Jones, *End of White Christianity in America.*

Part III: **Controversial Issues in Contemporary Missions/Missiology**

THREE BARRIERS LIE BETWEEN today's Evangelicals and an evangelical future. Having coursed their way through some of the major thinking and events of church history and world mission, it should not be difficult for readers to determine what those barriers are. They have to do with the trustworthiness of the Bible, the critical importance of orthodox creeds/confessions, and the meaning of mission. As it is, fundamental questions having to do with these three issues keep coming to the fore in one form or another, receive some attention, and then are gently laid to rest until some individual and/or occasion calls for their reconsideration. But they are almost invariably laid to rest without resolution. Closure is seldom sought and, of course, hardly ever achieved.

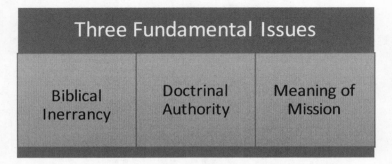

Figure 8. Contemporary evangelical missiology

As regrettable as that may be, lack of closure will necessarily be the case here and for obvious reasons. In part three we will deal with controversies in the evangelical movement over time. First in chapter 7 we deal with the three controversies mentioned above, then in chapter 8 with several proposals of front-running theologians/missiologists over the last generation that can be considered divisive and illustrative. Both sides—the pros and cons—of these proposals will be considered, but closure, if it comes at all, will have to await another time and place.

Chapter 7

Three Unavoidable Issues in Contemporary Evangelical Missiology

EVEN A CURSORY READING of the history of post-World War II Evangelicalism brings to light developments that are something of an embarrassment to a movement that was launched in part on the basis that their fundamentalist predecessors were both divisive and divided. It is important that younger Evangelicals especially know and understand the earlier goings-on that helped pave the way for the three basic issues that distinguish modern and postmodern Evangelicalism from the fundamentalism and early conservative Evangelicalism that preceded it.

The Inspiration and Authority of the Bible: Inerrancy and Infallibility

The so-called "battle for the Bible" should be part of the understanding of all Evangelicals. Not only was the "battle" itself important, over time its aftermath has taken some curious turns that cannot but have their own outworkings in the near or more distant future.

Infallibilism: The Fuller Seminary Story

Fuller Seminary was founded in 1947 and named after the famed fundamentalist speaker on the popular radio program "The Old-Fashioned Revival Hour," Charles E. Fuller. In the 1950s, certain faculty members came to believe that the Bible may contain errors of a scientific, geographical, or historical type. As a result the seminary finally removed the doctrine of inerrancy from its statement of faith in 1967. Ten years later, having come to believe that defection from inerrancy had invaded not only Fuller but other schools as well, Harold Lindsell published his book *The Battle for the Bible*.[1] Also about the same time, in response to Lindsell and his conservativism, Fuller's Jack Rogers edited *Biblical Authority* (1977) and, with Donald McKim, wrote *The Authority and Interpretation of the Bible: An Historical Approach* (1979). In these they argued that biblical inerrancy doctrine was a product of the late seventeenth century.

The background to all of this was as follows. Originally Fuller's doctrinal statement contained a statement to the effect that the Bible is "free from all error in the whole and in the part." But when Charles Fuller's son, Daniel Fuller (later, dean of the seminary), returned from studies under the famed neo-orthodox theologian Karl Barth in Switzerland, things began to change. Daniel Fuller maintained that the Bible contains not one but two types of literature. One part has to do with spiritual and moral teaching and is divinely inspired and infallible. Another part, having to do with science, geography, and history, on the other hand, may or may not be divinely inspired and may or may not be without error.

Some outstanding Fuller faculty members took issue with this and resigned, but over a period of years faculty members opting for the new position gained the upper hand. So when David L. Hubbard became president, the doctrinal statement was changed to read that the Bible is "infallible in those matters relating to faith and practice."

---

1. Lindsell, *Battle for the Bible*.

Attempting to state Fuller's position in a way that would appeal to a wide swath of Evangelicals, in 1979 Hubbard authored and Fuller Seminary published the book *What We Evangelicals Believe: Expositions of Christian Doctrine Based on "The Statement of Faith" of Fuller Theological Seminary*. Dealing with the difference between inerrancy and Fuller's type of infallibilist doctrine, Hubbard wrote,

> More recently, attention has been called to differences among evangelicals in the emphasis put on the inerrancy of Scripture or in the definition of inerrancy. There are some for whom a meticulous definition of inerrancy is an absolute essential for biblical faith, and there are others who feel that the focus on the details of science, geography, and history distracts us from the saving message and the spiritual teaching of Scripture.[2]

Hubbard goes on to quote the relevant paragraph in the new Fuller statement of faith itself as follows: "All of the books of the Old and New Testaments, given by divine inspiration, are the written word of God, the only infallible rule of faith and practice."[3] Readers will note that this says nothing to the effect that parts of the Bible may *not* be the "written word of God, the only infallible rule of faith and practice," although that was precisely the new meaning of "infallibility" in the Fuller view.

Inerrancy: The Trinity Evangelical Divinity School Story

By the mid-1960s one of a number of evangelical seminaries with a reputation for conservative theology was the seminary of the Evangelical Free Church of America (soon to be called Trinity Evangelical Divinity School) in Deerfield, Illinois. Neither the seminary nor the associated college were growing, however, and both faced an uncertain future financially. Denominational leaders became encouraged about the possibility of breathing new life

2. Hubbard, *What We Evangelicals Believe*, 13–14.
3. Hubbard, *What We Evangelicals Believe*, 18.

into the seminary especially and, at the same time, hoisting ever higher the flag of an inerrant and fully authoritative Bible. They wisely approached the situation as an opportunity to enhance the position of the seminary especially and, at the same time, reinforce the ranks of those contending for inerrancy of the Bible. They approached the Wheaton Graduate School's systematic theologian, Kenneth S. Kantzer, with an offer to become the new dean and an opportunity to assemble an interdenominational faculty of national and international reputation.

It would be a "match made in heaven." Historically, the Free Church stood for inerrancy (the answer to even minor disputes being itself a question: "Where stands it written?") and was known for its commitment to fulfilling the Great Commission and highlighting the Second Coming of Christ. On the larger evangelical scene, it had become apparent that churches, schools, and missions needed a fresh infusion of just that kind of conservative scholarship.

Like Daniel Fuller, Harvard graduate Kenneth Kantzer had also studied under Karl Barth in Switzerland. He knew well those particular issues that stemmed from continental liberalism and neo-orthodoxy, and he knew personally many of the most outstanding scholars engaged in the debate. At almost the precise time that David Hubbard was appointed president of Fuller, Kenneth Kantzer assumed Trinity's deanship and began to recruit his faculty—Old Testament scholar Gleason Archer and New Testament scholar Wilbur Smith from Fuller (and, later, systematic theologian Carl F. H. Henry and anthropologist Paul Hiebert); Walter Liefeld and Walter Kaiser from Wheaton; John Warwick Montgomery from St. Louis; Robert D. Culver from Northwestern; and special lecturers such as J. Oliver Buswell II and John Gerstner.

In that connection and in light of later events, it would be well to point out that regular faculty members were bound not only by the faith statements of their respective churches and denominations, but also by the faith statement of the Evangelical

Free Church.[4] Article I of the doctrinal statement of the Evangelical Free Church read as follows:

> We believe that God has spoken in the Scriptures, both Old and New Testaments, through the words of human authors. As the verbally inspired Word of God, the Bible is without error in the original writings, the complete revelation of His will for salvation, and the ultimate authority by which every realm of human knowledge and endeavor should be judged. Therefore it is to be believed in all that it teaches, obeyed in all that it requires, and trusted in all that it promises.[5]

And so the "battle for the Bible" was enjoined. Trinity faculty assumed active roles in the International Council of Biblical Inerrancy in the 1970s and some participated in the preparation of "The Chicago Statement on Biblical Inerrancy" (1978). Norman Geisler edited the book *Inerrancy* (1979).[6] John Woodbridge argued convincingly against the proposal of Rogers and McKim in his *Biblical Authority: A Critique of the Rogers/McKim Proposal* (1982)[7]—namely, that inerrancy is a more or less recent doctrine and not part of the classic legacy of the Christian church.

The Relative Importance of Doctrine and Experience: Traditionalism and Meliorism

According to Gerald McDermott the division between meliorists and traditionalists in today's evangelical movement is both deep

4. That statement has subsequently been modified somewhat and officially adopted at the Annual Conference of the Evangelical Free Church of America. It is equally strong in both the original and modified forms when it comes to Scripture, the new statement saying that "as the verbally inspired Word of God, the Bible is without error in the original writings, the complete revelation of His will for salvation, and the ultimate authority by which every realm of human knowledge and endeavor should be judged." "EFCA Statement of Faith," para. 2.

5. Olson, *This We Believe*, 181.

6. Geisler, *Inerrancy*.

7. Woodbridge, *Biblical Authority*.

and wide, and fully capable of bringing evangelicalism as we have known it to a final parting of the ways.[8]

Meliorism and Traditionalism Defined and Described

In McDermott's usage of the term, meliorist theologians prioritize experience over doctrine: "Orthopraxy is 'prior to' orthodoxy; the main purpose of revelation is transformation 'rather than' information; and doctrine is 'secondary' to evangelical experience."[9]

McDermott seems to agree with Kevin Vanhoozer when the latter says that there has been too much "wrangling over whether evangelicalism is a matter of doctrine or piety, the head or the heart."[10] Nevertheless, as theology has evolved, that distinction is at the core of a critical divide in contemporary evangelicalism. The old division between "Arminian synergism" (our wills cooperate with God's will in salvation and sanctification) and "Reformed monergism" (God's will determines ours without making us into robots) has now morphed into something much larger and more divisive—namely, in opposing groups of theologians. One group is composed of meliorists such as Roger E. Olson, Steve Chalke, Brian McLaren, Clark Pinnock, and Tony Campolo, and the other is composed of traditionalists such as Carl F. H. Henry, Kenneth Kantzer, J. I. Packer, D. A. Carson, Norman Geisler, Alister McGrath, and Thomas Oden.

It might be well to point out that all traditionalists are not alike, at least according to meliorist Roger Olson. He divides traditionalists into two camps: "biblicists," who see revelation as primarily propositional and doctrine as the essence of Christian faith, and "paleo-orthodox," who regard ancient ecumenical consensus as the governing authority in the interpretation of Scripture.[11] Taken together, biblicists and paleo-orthodox comprise the traditionalist

8. McDermott, "Emerging Divide."
9. McDermott, "Emerging Divide," 366.
10. Vanhoozer, "Lost in Interpretation?," 89.
11. McDermott, "Emerging Divide," 364.

stream of contemporary evangelicalism. For both "camps," *ortho-doxy is not only prior to orthopraxy but productive of it; Christian faith is not only prior to Christian living but gives rise to it.*

The biblicist and paleo-orthodox distinction aside, McDermott sums up the differences between traditionalists and meliorists as he sees them in the following way:

> It turns out then, at the end of the day, that what finally divides evangelical theologians today is their attitude toward tradition and Scripture. Meliorists say the historic church's understanding of Scripture should be scrutinized warily. Some of them profess respect for the Great Tradition, but because of their slippery approach to biblical inspiration and the subordination of doctrine to experience, their relation to that Tradition is tenuous. Because the meaning of the Word is found not in the words of the Bible but in the theology of the Meliorist interpreter, *sola scriptura* can become—despite the best intentions of its leading thinkers—*sola theologia*, with the charismatic theologian the final authority. Traditionalists, on the other hand, also affirm *sola scriptura*. Scripture is primary, but the great Tradition is the authoritative guide to its interpretation. Because they see doctrine and experience not above or below but inextricably bound up in one another, they allow the Great Tradition a veto. They yield far more often to that authority. They are ready, as Meliorists are not, to say that not only the words of Scripture but also significant segments of the unfolding of the Great Tradition were guided by the Spirit.[12]

The Problem with Meliorism

From McDermott's point of view (and from mine as well), the fundamental problem with prioritizing experience over tradition is that meliorists feel that creeds and creedal-like statements are man-made. They constitute tradition, and tradition is always in

12. McDermott, "Emerging Divide," 369.

need of reform. McDermott suggests that evangelicals take note of four melioristic tendencies:

1. Despite avowed respect for the great tradition, meliorists treat it with ambivalence. Tradition always needs correction and even the great tradition (including the Apostles' and Nicene Creeds and the Chalcedonian consensus) never is allowed to veto meliorist ideas.

2. Meliorists exalt experience at the expense of cognitive understanding (doctrine). That is dangerous. Christian beliefs are not rationalistic, but they are reasonable.

3. Meliorists often hesitate to support the plenary inspiration of Scripture, though they ordinarily insist on the authority of Scripture over tradition.

4. The foregoing tendencies add up to a lack of external authority. Authority is granted to scholars who have knowledge of ancient cultures and to charismatic meliorist scholars and writers.

In short, it's not so much what the Bible has said to our forefathers and teachers of long ago but what it says to you and me in the here and now that is important—even "final"—for the meliorist. And it may not be so much what the Bible and great tradition say to non-Christian cultures that is relevant—it may be what the Bible and great tradition say *as interpreted by cross-cultural specialists and responded to by indigenous hearers that is relevant.* This too is in accord with meliorism.

Mission as World Evangelization or Social Action: Prioritism and Holism

What is the meaning of the Christian mission? That is a basic and—for Christians at least—an all-important question. And yet, even two highly placed mission historians as gifted and knowledgeable as Charles Van Engen and Ralph Winter have answered it very differently.

Writing in 2010, Fuller Seminary's Charles Van Engen reluctantly discloses his stipulated definition of mission. He writes,

> I've been working on that [i.e., a definition of "mission"]
> for about 40 years now. Thus far in my own search for
> a definition I have arrived at the following tentative at-
> tempt: "God's mission works primarily through Jesus
> Christ's sending the people of God to intentionally cross
> barriers from church to nonchurch, faith to nonfaith, to
> proclaim by word and deed the coming of the Kingdom
> of God in Jesus reconciling people to God, to themselves,
> to one another, and to the world and gathering them into
> the church, through repentance and faith in Jesus Christ,
> by the work of the Holy Spirit, with a view to the trans-
> formation of the world, as a sign of the coming of the
> kingdom in Jesus Christ."[13]

Van Engen adds that this is not necessarily his final definition. He continues to work on it after forty years in the making and
may make further changes!

Writing ten years previously in 1998, Ralph Winter had written as follows:

> *The future of the world hinges on what we make of this*
> *word "mission."* Yet at this moment it is almost univer-
> sally misunderstood—in both liberal and conservative
> circles. About the only people who still think of mis-
> sion as having to do with preaching the gospel where
> Christ is not named, with being a testimony to the very
> last tribe and nation and tongue on this earth, are the
> often confused people in the pew. *In this matter their*
> *instincts outshine those of many eminent theologials [sic]*
> *and ecclesiastical statesmen.*[14]

Interestingly, Winter says nothing about rethinking and re-
vising his definition, though he is the one who, by the time Van
Engen discloses his definition of mission, will have made a revision

---

13. Van Engen, "'Mission' Defined and Described," 27.

14. Winter, "Meaning of 'Mission,'" 33–34 (first emphasis in original; second emphasis mine).

that goes beyond what Van Engen proposes. More on that later. Here I call attention only to the fact that these two diverse definitions illustrate two very different ways in which contemporary evangelicals describe and define the mission of the church. Some such as Van Engen define mission widely, incorporating as much as plausible of the missionary thinking and doings of the church down through history, especially modern history. *Theologically and practically, mission is "inclusive"; it is "holistic."*

Winter's early (1998) description/definition, on the other hand, exhibits a more traditional conservative understanding. In brief, Christian mission is world evangelization. Elaborated somewhat, it has to do with discipling the world's peoples and organizing believers into churches—churches which, in turn, will help carry forward the mission of the church. Mission includes humanitarian endeavors but as secondary and supporting of the main task. Mission is prioritistic.

Overall and for a number of reasons, evangelical missions like their ecumenical counterparts have tended to become more inclusivistic and holistic over recent years. I think that that is not in question. What is in question is how long this process can continue if evangelical missions are to remain "evangelical."

Chapter 8

Decisive Differences between Prominent Evangelical Theologians and Missiologists

Turning now from the three controversial issues that have divided theologians and missiologists in recent years, we want to consider several representative but potentially equally divisive individual proposals. One has to do with George Eldon Ladd's well-known inaugurated eschatology. Another has to do with Kevin Vanhoozer's lesser known critique of the so-called "Hodge-Henry hypothesis." And the third one has to do with the new view of the kingdom as proposed by Ralph Winter in years prior to his homegoing.

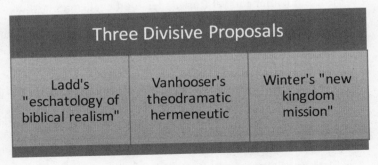

Figure 9. Some evangelical proposals in theology and mission

I do not deny that these three proposals are brilliantly conceived and forwarded by outstanding scholars of church and mission. That, as a matter of fact, is part of the reason that I have chosen to deal with them here. But at the same time, I would suggest that any one of these proposals is sufficiently radical to sever evangelicalism from its moorings in Scripture and the great tradition of Christian thinking.

Several of those scholars mentioned in this chapter have, or have had, faculty positions at Trinity and that calls for information beyond the usual. As recently as 2014, Trinity's Scott Manetsch reviewed the Fuller/Trinity story related in chapter 7 above[1] and suggested that Trinity became popular in the 1960s and 1970s for a number of reasons, among them Trinity's "commitment to examine controversial theological and intellectual issues of the day in a manner both fair and biblically responsible." Now it is fairly well known that the Evangelical Free Church (and therefore Trinity as well) has made some changes in its statement of faith in recent years. Change involves controversy, so we can anticipate that controversy will affect what we have to say about TEDS faculty as well as outsiders.

George Eldon Ladd's "Eschatology of Biblical Realism"

After the passing of more than a generation since he proposed it, George Eldon Ladd's "eschatology of biblical realism" is still one of the most influential and yet least understood challenges to traditional eschatologies circulating among evangelicals.

Ladd's "Eschatology of Biblical Realism"

In 1974, Ladd republished his 1964 book *Jesus and the Kingdom*, under the title *The Presence of the Future: The Eschatology of Biblical Realism*.[2] The book soon gained widespread notoriety. Ladd

---

1. Cf. Manetsch, *Trinity Evangelical Divinity School*.
2. Ladd, *Presence of the Future*.

proposed a synthesis between futuristic and present aspects of Christ's kingdom. According to Ladd, our missionary message, like the message of Jesus, is the gospel of the kingdom—the *good news* of God's redemptive acts in history and the fact that the *reign of God has already broken into the affairs of men*.[3] Kingdom *power* today is the same as that demonstrated by Jesus in his authority over sickness and evil spirits. Its *promise* is the promise of the kingdom of God—all the blessings of divine rule. The kingdom's *presence* was inaugurated by Jesus and involves two movements: first, a fulfillment *within* history; second, a consummation at the *end* of history.

Ladd considers the church to be a "society of men" displaying humanness as much or more than divine rulership. God's kingdom is at work in the world as much or more than it is at work in the church. The kingdom is not so much a *domain* as it is the *dominion* of Christ. Where he is, there is the kingdom. The mission is not to *build* the kingdom but, rather, to witness to its outworking in this present world. The crucial "breaking in" of God's rulership attended the coming and ministry of Jesus and, therefore, "before the eschatological appearing of God's Kingdom at the end of the age, God's Kingdom has become dynamically active among men in Jesus' person and mission."[4]

Culver's "Greater Commission"

Kenneth Kantzer's choice to head the department of systematic theology at Trinity in the middle sixties was Robert Culver. Culver's dispensational eschatology was almost the same as that of the Evangelical Free Church with the exception that Culver believed that the apostles had fulfilled the Great Commission, and the church's "Greater Commission" was identical with the commission of the apostle Paul in Romans 10. Culver's book on the subject is

---

3. Ladd, *Presence of the Future*, 267.
4. Ladd, *Presence of the Future*, 139.

entitled *A Greater Commission,* which, due to publishing delays at Moody Press, was not published until 1984.[5]

To elaborate somewhat on Culver's view of the kingdom and mission, he believed that the Gospel of Matthew is the divine blueprint for church and mission and, to a degree, for Great Commission mission. Instead of "*As you go* make disciples of all nations" as the Lord Jesus had instructed the apostles in Matt 28:19a, however, the Lord gave Paul—and by extension, the Christian church—a "greater commission" in Rom 10:14–15.[6] Christ was sent into the world by the Father. The apostles were sent into the world by Christ. Christians are *already in the world.* They are to be salt and light and, as they go about in the world, they are to make disciples. *But, beyond that, there is a special "human sending" of and by Christ's people: namely, some must go, and those who do not go must send others.* Take special note: it's not "as you go" or "when you go," but "you go, or you send others." As Culver says,

> Christians must do more than simply *take the gospel along* wherever they go. . . . Paul proposed that Christians should also mount campaigns of evangelism; they must dedicate life and treasure *to send* gospel messengers to foreign parts, and some Christians must *go.*[7]

"At the Surface" and "Digging Deeper"

Much is going on here—some parts of it very evident, some parts of it outside that which readers will ordinarily be privy to.

In effect, Ladd's "eschatology of biblical realism" represents a kind of "in-between" eschatology bridging and mediating between apocalyptic eschatology and realized eschatology, between a social gospel and a spiritual gospel, between dispensational theology and covenant theology. It has elicited both praise and blame from all sides—but mainly praise even from some conservative evangelicals.

---

5. Culver, *Greater Commission.*

6. Culver, *Greater Commission,* 119.

7. Culver, *Greater Commission,* 126 (emphasis in original).

That may be due in part to the fact that some of Ladd's writings have been featured in the course materials of the popular Perspectives on the World Christian Movement. It should be mentioned, however, Perspectives' treatment does not dig very deeply into the meaning and implications of Ladd's eschatology. My experience with the course leads me to believe that most students and many, if not most, lecturers are not at all aware of Ladd's view of Scripture authority and its impact on his interpretation.

On that score it is worth noting that Ladd's biographer, Donald Reid, says that *The Presence of the Future* "was intended to bring him [Ladd] the cherished recognition of the broader community of biblical scholars."[8] An indication that that "cherished recognition" might have been achieved at a price is found in Ladd's openness to the methods of modern criticism, including the prominent liberal idea that the book of Daniel is a collection of "traditions" that relate to "*allegedly*" historical events.[9]

Culver's work is in harmony with Ladd at some points. In fact he commends Ladd's 1974 original edition of *The Presence of the Future* and includes it in his bibliography. There is no indication that he investigated Ladd's subsequent writings. As a matter of fact, the differences between the two are profound. In contrast to Ladd, Culver (1) subscribed to the integrity of the whole of Scripture (including the book of Daniel) and the necessity of a grammatico-historical hermeneutic; (2) took Daniel's images and visions with utmost seriousness and interpreted them as being the Divine blueprint for end time events; (3) believed the church to be the one body on earth where the rulership of Christ should be most evident; (4) taught that believers are, first and foremost, witnesses to Christ and messengers of the gospel as articulated in John 3:16; and (5) insisted that the mission of the church is the same as that of the apostle Paul.

That is not all, however. The Evangelical Free Church as a whole—and what is now called Trinity International University (includes the Divinity School and the College)—as part of it, has

8. Reid, "George Eldon Ladd," 627.

9. Ladd, *Presence of the Future*, 85, 95.

in recent years removed both the word "imminent" and premi-
llennialist eschatology from its statement of faith as we have indicated. One can only conjecture as to what that might mean for
the future. But the eschatology of the future is more likely to be
of the type proposed by Ladd than the traditional dispensational
kind espoused by Culver.

Kevin Vanhoozer's "Theodramatic Hermeneutic"

Coming up to postmodern times, at the annual meeting of the
Evangelical Theological Society held in San Antonio in 2004, the
current research professor in Trinity's department of systematic
theology, Kevin Vanhoozer, delivered a substantive and somewhat
startling plenary paper entitled "Lost in Interpretation? Truth,
Scripture, and Hermeneutics." A somewhat modified version of
the paper was published in the *Journal of the Evangelical Theological Society* the following year.[10] What follows here is not meant to
be a summary of the paper, but represents an attempt to point out
some included proposals that, if adopted, would certainly impact
both evangelical schools and missions.

Vanhoozer's Postconservative Position on
Biblical Authority and Interpretation

It aids understanding to realize from the beginning that Vanhoozer
does not hesitate to being identified as "postconservative" and that
he defines postconservatism as follows:

> By "postconservative" I understand an approach that,
> while recognizing the propositional component of
> speech acts, does not reduce language to reference or the
> cognitive dimension of theology to propositional state-
> ments. A postconservative theology affirms a *plurality of
> normative points of view in Scripture,* each of which is

10. Vanhoozer, "Lost in Interpretation?"

authoritative because each discloses a particular *aspect* of the truth.[11]

Vanhoozer's postconservatism is wary of what he deems to be an overemphasis on cognitive and propositional theology in general and biblical theology in particular. In addition to accepting differing interpretations of the biblical text as normative, his postconservatism yields the following proposals.

1. The truth of Scripture is mainly personal/relational rather than propositional/doctrinal. Vanhoozer says that Carl F. H. Henry subscribed to the doctrine of the inspiration and authority of Scripture advocated by Charles Hodge and Benjamin Warfield in the late nineteenth century. In his paper, Vanhoozer refers to that doctrine as the "Hodge-Henry hypothesis"—a hypothesis which he characterizes and disavows. He says that, according to the "Hodge-Henry hypothesis,"

   > [Christian] doctrine is the result of biblical induction and deduction, a capsule summary of the meaning of Scripture "taken as a set of propositional statements, each expressing a divine affirmation, valid always and everywhere." Propositionalist theology tends to see Scripture in terms of revelation, revelation in terms of conveying information, and theology in terms of divine information-processing.[12]

   Vanhoozer believes that the future of evangelicalism may depend on how it answers the question "Is the truth of Scripture personal/relational or propositional/doctrinal?"[13] He agrees that biblical truth is propositional and doctrinal, but he goes on to say that "the truth of the Bible lays claim not only to our heads but to our hearts and our hands."[14] He believes that the inerrancy position of even some of the most prominent and influential inerrantists is deficient in this

11. Vanhoozer, "Lost in Interpretation?," 108n58 (emphasis in original).

12. Vanhoozer, "Lost in Interpretation?," 95.

13. Vanhoozer, "Lost in Interpretation?," 93.

14. Vanhoozer, "Lost in Interpretation?," 110.

regard. For example, he calls the "Hodge-Henry hypothesis" a "cheap inerrancy" presumably because it lays claim primarily to our heads and satisfies itself with stating and holding to propositions of the faith quite apart from their practice.[15]

2. The inerrancy of the Bible is best understood as mapping out an *itinerary* that leads to Christ. The Bible is wholly true and trustworthy in the classical sense of "infallibility," i.e., "its *direction* is totally reliable."[16] "Perhaps," writes Vanhoozer, "we need to rehabilitate that classic term in order to make sure that theological interpreters of Scripture do not become mere information processors."[17]

3. The best method of Scripture interpretation is the "theodramatic." Vanhoozer posits a kind of hermeneutic that affirms much of the Bible that conservative inerrantists have interpreted very differently and, according to Vanhoozer, very often wrongly. Vanhoozer follows second-generation Barthians such as Hans Frei and George Lindbeck at this point. While Carl Henry, for example, is committed to truth as historical factuality, for Frei "it is the biblical narrative itself, not its propositional paraphrase, that is the truth-bearer."[18] "Whereas for Henry," Vanhoozer writes, "doctrines state the meaning of the narratives, for Frei we only understand the doctrine by understanding the story."[19]

It follows that a "theodramatic hermeneutic" is all about "*theodrama*—the words and deeds of God on the stage of world history that climax in Jesus Christ."[20] God uses propositional revelation to establish covenantal relations as much as to convey

---

15. Vanhoozer, "Lost in Interpretation?," 99.
16. Vanhoozer, "Lost in Interpretation?," 113.
17. Vanhoozer, "Lost in Interpretation?," 115.
18. Vanhoozer, "Lost in Interpretation?," 99.
19. Vanhoozer, "Lost in Interpretation?," 99.
20. Vanhoozer, "Lost in Interpretation?," 100–101.

information. Doctrine is *"direction for our fitting participation in the drama of redemption."*[21] In Vanhoozer's words,

> Doctrinal truth thus becomes a matter of *theodramatic correspondence* between our words and deeds and God's words and deeds. Theodramatic correspondence means life and language that is *in accord with* the gospel and *according to* the Scriptures. We speak and do the truth when our words and actions display theodramatic "fittingness."[22]

Jerry M. Ireland: Reinterpreting Carl F. H. Henry

Carl Henry has always embraced the kind of mission that involves both true words and good deeds—the regeneration of both man and society. Accordingly, his "Regenerational Model of Evangelism and Social Concern" has therefore been both rightly and rigorously defended by Assembly of God missionary Jerry M. Ireland. Ireland attempts to show that Henry's position has been misunderstood by many and that, rightly interpreted, Henry is making a cogent case for consensus between evangelical prioritists and holists. In short, Ireland says that, according to Henry, the basic problem in the prioritistic–holistic controversy is that advocates on both sides read too much into the meaning of the respective terms "holistic" and "prioritistic." Consensus is possible if both sides can agree on terminology "that captures the ultimate nature of evangelism as a *macro priority*, along with the *necessary nature* of social concern" as having a spiritual dimension.[23]

Ireland is perhaps correct, but his resolution of the problem seems overly simplistic. It barely hints at most of Vanhoozer's concerns, which may be wrong but are hardly simple. Though his choice of words is somewhat different (e.g., "macro priority'" and "necessary nature" instead of "primary task" and "supporting ministries"), Ireland's solution to the age-old question "Which is the most important?" is deficient in that the problem is really

21. Vanhoozer, "Lost in Interpretation?," 102 (emphasis in original).

22. Vanhoozer, "Lost in Interpretation?," 102 (emphasis in original).

23. Ireland, "Henry's Regenerational Model," 51–73.

theological, not semantic. And irony of ironies, it seems to me that Ireland's answer is much the same as the traditional evangelical answer: evangelism and humanitarianism; gospel words and good works; ministry to the soul and spirit, and ministry to the mind and body—they all go together.

But, again, which is most important—words or works? Like questions on the authority of Scripture and the meaning of the biblical text, some theologians/missiologists will answer one way, some the other. Hopefully, we can get it right in the future.

Ralph Winter: "A New Kingdom Mission"

We were good friends, Ralph Winter and I. And we agreed on many of the basics including the meaning of mission. That is, we agreed on the meaning of mission right up until and including Winter's 1998 definition of mission which we have just considered (see p. 93 above). But we did not agree following a consultation held in Techny, Illinois, on October 23–24, 2006. The consultation included evangelical scholars representing various professions and was called with the express purpose of discussing and evaluating Winter's "radically different interpretation of the Lord's Prayer and the Great Commission" which was at the heart of his "crucially deeper understanding" of the Christian mission.[24]

Succinctly stated, Winter's "deeper understanding of mission" in this postmodern globalized world was that mission requires us to do more than preach what he refers to as the "simple gospel of saving souls and planting churches." The "gospel" in the New Testament usually refers to the gospel of the kingdom, and the "kingdom gospel" requires that Christians meet basic human needs for education, food, water, medicine, justice, and peace. In fact, mission does not end even there. It also requires us to undertake the kind of organized research and endeavors that combat evil in all its forms—violence, injustice, poverty, environmental exploitation, international development, human and drug-trafficking, and

24. Winter, "ESSAY 3," 164–91.

disease—even efforts aimed at the restoration of vicious animals to their original non-carnivorous state, and efforts aimed at the eradication of disease-bearing microbes.[25]

The response to Winter's new definition of mission in Techny, October 2006 was as cool as autumn weather in Illinois. But Winter's prominence as founder of the US Center for World Mission, William Carey International University, William Carey Library, and the Perspectives movement tended to deflect criticism and assure a minimum of criticism if not a modicum of agreement. I include an elaboration of his new understanding here for a number of reasons but mainly because it is unique and illustrates how radically even a leading scholar and avid promoter of Christian mission can change his or her mind in a brief period of time.

Some Precursors and Components of Winter's New "Kingdom Mission"

Two things any critic could have anticipated when contending with Ralph Winter on an issue—first, he was well prepared, and second, he was tenacious in a friendly sort of way. Winter and I had a long period of correspondence on his changed view comprising some forty-nine exchanges of email notes and letters. I was not able to convince him of error on any point of importance. But the exchange did not diminish our friendship in Christ one iota. It did extend my understanding, but it did not change my view. According to Ralph Winter,

1. God created and endowed Satan with the extraordinary capacity actually to initiate sin and suffering in all their multifarious forms. His special focus on the destruction of disease-bearing microbes likely grew out of his own experience.

2. Building on Merrill Unger and a "contemporary scientific consensus," Winter understood complex life to have evolved over perhaps five hundred million years, the great bulk of which were characterized by great violence, massive eruptions, and

25. Winter, "ESSAY 3," 178–87.

a series of cataclysmic "extinction events" triggered by collisions of asteroids with our earth. All of this preceded Gen 1:1 and resulted in the destruction of most life and the generally chaotic condition of the whole world, including that part of the world dealt with in the Genesis account.

3. Winter's new understanding rested squarely on his interpretation of history—biblical history, of course, but also the history of church and mission. Winter took special note of the part played by post-Reformation "First- and Second-Inheritance Evangelicalism" in the ongoing "kingdom war" between God and Satan. "First-Inheritance Evangelicalism" was characterized by a dual emphasis on the earthly and heavenly, the social and the personal. In America it branched into two "reductionisms." One reductionism among upper-class influential Christians emphasized social concern—God's will on *earth*. A second reductionism (i.e., "Second-Inheritance Evangelicalism") emphasized personal salvation coupled with an otherworldly focus on *heaven*. This second reductionism, represented by evangelist D. L. Moody and theologian C. I. Scofield, became mainstream evangelicalism in America. It labeled those who exercised social concern as liberals, eschewed the word "kingdom," and evolved a theology of "this world is not my home, I'm just a passin' through." It elaborated into the Bible school movement, and the Bible schools educated the majority of evangelical missionaries, especially during the early twentieth century. Only recently has evangelicalism attained social influence through the conversion of Bible schools into colleges and universities.

4. Winter believed that "First-Inheritance Evangelicalism" coming from both Catholic and Protestant traditions and, especially, Great Awakening developments resulted in the word "evangelical" referring to something more than correct belief. It came to refer to individuals who had a personal "evangelical experience," not just those who mentally assent to some sort of intellectual creed. He also asserted that "it would be impossible

to overstate the significant changes of direction of both the Christian movement and our nation between 1815 and 1850,"[26] such as the banning of alcoholic beverages by most states in response to the work of the temperance movement and the momentum gained by the abolitionist movement—both prior to 1850. Winter concludes that, *employing the tools made available by contemporary science, "Kingdom Mission" is eminently achievable in our world and that is what the church should be working for and praying for.*

The Contrary Opinion of Two among Many

Winter's new view is so many-sided and incorporates arguments from so many sources religious and secular that to attempt a critique of substance here would constitute an injustice both to him and to his theory. But in a more recently published book, *MissionShift: Global Mission Issues in the Third Millennium,*[27] in a critique of holism in general, prioritist Christopher R. Little[28] makes a special point of the fact that when Winter proposes that missionaries use scientific methods to "'*destroy all forms of evil, both human and microbiological,' he is compounding the problem.*"[29] I agree. Contrary to Winter it seems to me that when Christians pray "Thy Kingdom come" they are not praying for success in employing science to establish the Kingdom, they are praying for the coming of the King!

Closing Reflections

Now think back to the dialogue between liberal David L. Edwards and evangelical John R. W. Stott which we referred to at the very beginning of this book. According to Stott, since the

26. Winter, "ESSAY 3," 173–74.

27. Hesselgrave and Stetzer, *MissionShift.*

28. Little, "In Response," 212.

29. Winter, "ESSAY 3," 190.

liberal resembles a gas-filled balloon unrestrained by confession and creed, he is free to take off and rise in the air "buoyant, free, directed only by [his] own navigational responses . . . entirely unrestrained from earth."[30]

On the other hand and also according to Stott, the evangelical resembles a kite which can take off, "fly great distances and soar to great heights, while all the time being tethered to earth."[31] He goes on to say,

> For the Evangelical mind is held by revelation. Without doubt it often needs a longer string, for we are not renowned for creative thinking. Nevertheless, at least in the ideal, I see Evangelicals as finding true freedom under the authority of revealed truth, and combining a radical mind and lifestyle with a conservative commitment to Scripture.[32]

Now after reviewing the nuts and bolts of twentieth-century liberalism and evangelicalism in Part III, it must be apparent that, while Stott's metaphors and explanation are well conceived and generally true, if they are taken as the final word on any matter they can be misguided and even mistaken. Like liberals, though to a lesser degree, evangelicals do no small amount of "creative thinking"—if that is what it is rightly called. It is no longer sufficient to ask, "Where stands it written?" Only when evangelizing (and likely not even there) is it enough to say, "The Bible says . . ." "Inerrancy" and "infallibility" are being refined and redefined. Grammatico-historical exegesis is being rethought and replaced.

That much has become clear in preceding chapters. The question is, what should be done about it if we are to save an evangelical future? Modest answers to that question will be attempted in that which is yet to come.

---

30. Edwards and Stott, *Evangelical Essentials*, 106.

31. Edwards and Stott, *Evangelical Essentials*, 106.

32. Edwards and Stott, *Evangelical Essentials*, 106.

Part IV: **Faith for the Future**

PART IV IS ALL about faith—the faith once for all delivered to the saints; the faith found in the confessions and creeds of the early church, in the teachings of the Reformers, in the preaching of the Great Awakening; the faith that William Carey took to India, Adoniram Judson took to Burma, and Henry Martin took to China.

The questions to be addressed in part four have to do with the status of this faith especially in America: "How does the faith fare in our nation and in our schools, in our churches and in our missions?" With respect to the Christian mission, the nineteenth century is often thought of as the British century and the twentieth century as the American century. What about the twenty-first?

In his recent book *The End of White Christian America*, Robert P. Jones, founder of Public Religion Research Institute, writes that the decline of Christianity among white Christians in America has been "swift and dramatic"[1] and has occurred among evangelicals as well as the old mainline denominations. White evangelical Protestants comprised 22 percent of the population in 1988. That number had plummeted to 18 percent by 2016. In 1972 white Protestants' median age was forty-six years old; today it is fifty-three.[2]

1. Jones, *End of White Christian America*, 49.
2. Jones, *End of White Christian America*, 55.

In a recent article in the *New York Times*, author Ross Douthat writes about the aging of mainline Protestantism, the weakening of Catholicism, and the rise in the number of Americans who claim no religious affiliation whatsoever. He goes on to cite various scholars as to their views on Christianity in America today. Sociologist of religion Christian Smith characterizes the passing generation of evangelicals as being part of American modernity but also as living in tension with pluralistic and permissive values. However, Baylor professor Alan Jacobs sees many younger evangelicals as simply leaving the movement. Jared Wilson of the Gospel Coalition describes younger evangelicals as having become "theological orphans."[3] It is not a pretty picture.

On a different but related note, Notre Dame historian Mark Noll writes, "The evangelical traditions consistently maintain the major evangelical traits, *but they have done so with a tremendously diverse array of emphases, relationships and special concerns.*"[4] That is certainly and profoundly the case unless Noll is implying that the movement consistently maintains major emphases, relationships, and concerns that are not in need of conservative evangelical correctives. That would not be true. In fact, the contrary is true. Evangelicalism as we have come to know and experience it is in need of constant and consistent in-course correction.

Indeed, if evangelical churches are to survive, much less thrive, orthodox doctrine must be encouraged and embraced, and sub-orthodox doctrine must be recognized and resisted. That is what chapter 9 and the closing sections of this book are all about.

---

3. Douthat, "Is There an Evangelical Crisis?"
4. Noll, *Rise of Evangelicalism*, 20 (emphasis mine).

Chapter 9

The Evangelical Crisis and Its Resolution

ONCE AGAIN, I BELIEVE that a good case can be made for saying that the fundamental problem in evangelical churches and missions is a weakening of *the* faith—objective faith, revealed faith, the historic Christian faith, the faith of the church fathers. Over two generations ago in the 1980s, the International Council on Biblical Inerrancy (ICBI), one of evangelicalism's best hopes for holding the line against sub-orthodox theological/missiological proposals, folded its tent and disbanded altogether. By that time, two movements that became popular almost overnight—the Prayer and Praise movement and the Short-Term Missions movement—captured the commitment of churches and missions with theological and doctrinal consequences that have been slightly less than overwhelming and not altogether positive. Though there have been benefits that accrued through at least some of this, the result of all of it has not been altogether hopeful. In what follows we will explore the above along with a related topic, the Small Group Bible Study movement.

Figure 10. Doctrinal orthodoxy and contemporary
evangelical movements

The International Council on Biblical Inerrancy: Its
Contributions and the Consequences of Its Dissolution

One of the most popular evangelical apologist-theologians of the postwar period, Francis Schaeffer, predicted that the fortunes of the conservative evangelical movement were inextricably tied to the doctrine of inerrancy of Scripture.[1] He had a point, and he may prove to have been right. There can be little doubt but that with the demise of the ICBI and the failure of evangelicals to mount an organization of equal conservative influence, a major shift occurred.

The ICBI was formed in the 1970s. Its membership included well-known conservative evangelical scholars such as Kenneth Kantzer, J. I. Packer, D. A. Carson, Harold Lindsell, John Woodbridge, Roger Nicolle, and a large coterie of similarly well-known and equally influential scholars. It was unusually active and productive toward the end of the 1970s and throughout the 1980s, especially among conservative Lutherans but others as well.

Among the best-known contributions of the ICBI to the cause of inerrancy were the "The Chicago Statement on Biblical Inerrancy" in 1978 and a scholarly volume, *Inerrancy*, edited by Norman Geisler.[2] However, the council contributed far more than

1. Schaeffer, *Great Evangelical Disaster*.
2. Geisler, *Inerrancy*.

well-read publications. It provided an able and ready forum for debating the biblical validity or invalidity of proposals forwarded by notable scholars across the theological spectrum. As long as the International Council was alive and active, the inerrancy of the Bible autographs and their place in maintaining orthodoxy in the theological/scientific discussions and debates of the time was assured. When, however, in the 1980s leaders declared that the council had accomplished its purpose and that they had decided to dissolve it, the situation changed. Inerrancy was no longer attended by a ready slate of defenders, the larger inerrancy conversation was often neglected, and sub-orthodox expressions of missions/missiology often went unanswered. For my part, I believe that the council was actually dissolved because many of its leaders were approaching retirement age and were no longer able to keep up with the pace they had set for themselves.[3] In any case, there was plenty of work left to be done, but for whatever reason(s), conservative evangelicals had lost the focus required to carry on such a demanding effort.

After 1977, Jay Grimstead, who had played an important part in the formation and continuation of the International Council, took the lead in establishing two groups—the Coalition on Revival and the International Church Council Project. Grimstead and his colleagues had the specific goal of establishing an international consortium of evangelical theologians who would subscribe to and carry forward the foundational doctrines of the historic Christian church, including the doctrine of inerrancy.[4] The COR and ICCP are still active and productive, but they have never been able to fill the gaping hole left by the demise of the ICBI. In fact, as we have seen in our summaries of various entities of the evangelical movement, no evangelical entity has measured up to the ICBI standard when it comes to declaring and defending the complete truthfulness of the monographs of Scripture. Instead, a profound doctrinal irenicism tends to reign.

3. I came to this conclusion after a lengthy conversation with Roger Nicole. Nicole was well informed and highly concerned.

4. Grimstead and Clingman, *Rebuilding Civilization on the Bible*.

The Praise and Worship Movement

The popular Praise and Worship movement (sometimes, simply the Praise movement) got its start in the 1960s among the street people of southern California. It grew rapidly with the teaching and support of Pastor Chuck Smith of Calvary Chapel in Costa Mesa and Calvary's initiation of what came to be called the Maranatha Music Co (incorporated in December 1971).

Music has always been key to the growth of the movement. Street people were not "tuned" to organs and the conventional hymnody of the average church. In fact, one Calvary Chapel leader confesses that, after his conversion and before Calvary Chapel adopted the new style of music, he sometimes came late to services "just to avoid the music."[5] Not all praise music is of the same genre, but the new music nevertheless is usually tuned to the accompaniment of guitars, keyboards, and drums. It also features Scripture verses, simplicity, redundancy, and melodious tunes as they may pop into the head of the composer. Hymnals have been replaced by videos that allow for the frequent addition of new songs. That is important because praise songs are sometimes created spontaneously with lyrics being attached to melodies as far out as a Coca-Cola commercial.[6]

Today the outcomes of Praise movement music are almost everywhere evident throughout the churches in North America and well beyond. But change has not occurred without a fight. As Larry Eskridge writes,

> "Worship wars" have become a fact of life as traditionalists battle champions of the new music, often resulting in separate worship services or the uneasy compromise of "blended worship." As the debris has begun to settle and as generations have waxed and waned, it is clear that Protestant musical expression has irrevocably changed. While organs still intone "A Mighty Fortress" and congregations continue to sing just one more stanza of "Power in the Blood," a new set of "standards" such as

5. Eskridge, "'Praise and Worship' Revolution."
6. Eskridge, "'Praise and Worship' Revolution."

"He is Exalted" and "Shout to the Lord"—led by "worship teams" wielding guitars and electronic keyboards—have joined the ancient call to worship.[7]

Eskridge has put his finger on it. This intergenerational war has already been won in many churches, *but in some it is still being waged so there is still hope. The problem is not so much the guitars, keyboards, and commercial tunes as it is the lyrics created on the spot from biblical texts that pop into the minds of adepts who may be sincere but are often immature in their Christian faith. As even a cursory reading of the lyrics of more traditional hymns will show, Christian truth is much more replete with meaning and embraces more of the great tradition of Christian thinking.*

I hesitate to introduce a theological word such as "meliorism" into a discussion on the "the Praise movement." These are, however, next-door neighbors and get along extremely well together. And since meliorism is already part of our discussion—and an important part of it at that (see p. 89)—I think it well briefly to explore their relationship because of its importance to the future of church and mission.

Looking back we recall that for meliorist theologians and those who follow them, "doctrine is secondary to evangelical experience," "meliorists exalt experience at the expense of cognitive understanding," and "it's not so much what the Bible has said to our forefathers and teachers [in the past] but what it says to you and me in the here and now that is important—even 'final'—for the meliorist" (see pp. 89–92). Evangelicals need to think hard and long about this. The word "meliorism" is not at all well known, but its theology and practice are encountered often and regularly in many of our churches and missions. *The fact is that the close relationship between meliorist theologians and pastors on the one hand and meliorist musicians and missionaries on the other is not so much a matter of shared location as it is a matter of shared DNA. What is often made out to be an "intergenerational music war" turns*

---

7. Eskridge, "'Praise and Worship' Revolution."

out to be something other than—or something in addition to that. It is also part of a theological war!

A fundamental principle of the Christian faith is at stake here. The Holy Spirit did not inspire the apostle Paul to write, "Faith cometh by feeling and feeling by the worship of God." The Holy Spirit inspired Paul to write, "Faith cometh by hearing, and hearing by the Word of God" (Rom 10:17). And so it is, and so it will always be.

The Small Group Bible Study Movement

Small groups are intended to provide a setting where "specific needs can be met within the group as the Bible is applied to daily life."[8] And yet, while many positives accompany studying Scripture with fellow believers, this emphasis on biblically meeting practical needs within the group can disengage Bible study from a historical, theological basis.

In *No Place for Truth: Or Whatever Happened to Evangelical Theology?* David Wells argues that the disappearance of theology in evangelicalism is basically characterized by an "anti-theological" mood—often present in small group contexts—which severs its link to historical, Protestant orthodoxy. In the past, there were three essential aspects to "doing theology" in both the church and academy: 1) a confessional element, or the historic creeds which crystallize into doctrine; 2) careful reflection on this confession "to seek to understand the connections between what is confessed and what, in any given society, is taken as normative"; and 3) the cultivation of virtues which are grounded in the first two elements.[9] Carson, especially, shows the importance of integrating awareness of the history of doctrine (historical theology) with careful biblical exegesis, biblical theology, systematic theology, and pastoral theology in teaching about the "hermeneutical circle."[10]

8. Neumann, "Small Groups," 882.

9. Wells, *No Place for Truth*, 96–100.

10. For a description of D. A. Carson's theological methodology, see Naselli, "D. A. Carson's Theological Method."

Paralleling this "dismembering" of theology is the fact that, while the articles of belief are still professed, they are no longer at the center of what it means to be an evangelical, nor do they determine evangelical conduct. The modern "cult of self," with its emphasis on self-understanding and self-fulfillment, has poured into the resulting void. Among evangelicals, the ascendancy of what Wells calls "self-piety" has resulted in a psychologizing and subjectivizing of Christian faith. Emphasis is often placed on "what the passage means to me" and on exploring "inner feelings."

Much like Esau, who traded his birthright for a meal of bread and lentil stew, small group participants are at risk of partaking in a limited meal to the exclusion of a feast of nourishment they have inherited from spiritual forebears. Like a birthright, the great tradition has mattered from the beginning and its acceptance or denial puts much at stake for generations to come.

Short-Term Missions and Long-Term Consequences

The last generation has witnessed yet another movement—the Short-Term Missions movement (STM)—that is of such size and significance that it cannot but change the face of evangelical churches and missions for a long time to come. Starting with strategies employed by Operation Mobilization (OM) and Youth With a Mission (YWAM) in the 1960s and 1970s, Short-Term Missions has grown dramatically until today it actually dominates the lion's share of the attention and support of numerous churches, and not a few missions as well.

> More than a thousand U.S. mission organizations and ministries that we are aware of send people on short-term trips of one kind or another, in addition to the tens of thousands of churches and more than a thousand Christian colleges, seminaries and high schools that sponsor trips. Similar things are happening in Europe, Latin America, Australia, and a number of Asian countries. This great diversity among sending organizations, participants, destinations and models makes it difficult

to produce accurate estimates about how many people go on mission trips. Who can know?[11]

Based on national random survey data, sociologist Christian Smith concludes that 29 percent of all thirteen- to seventeen-year-olds in the United States have "gone on a religious missions team or religious service project," with 10 percent having gone on such trips three or more times. If so, well over two million thirteen- to seventeen-year-olds alone go on such trips every year.[12] About 60 percent of all short-termers are sent by their local church to work with people they know, not by parachurch groups or mission agencies as such. Some 35 percent of them work right here in the United States.[13]

The literature on short-term missions—of which there is much!—leaves one almost stupefied as to their accomplishments and value, and strengths and weaknesses, and even their desirability and undesirability. That is not for me to deal with here. I will leave all of that for my missiological colleagues to review and evaluate. Here I will simply assume that the overwhelming majority of short-termers who are willing to go to the time, effort, and expense of helping needy people somewhere in one way or another do just that—*they help needy people and that is good! My concern here is elsewhere.* David Dockery and Timothy George put their finger on it when they suggest that

> there are those in the churches who would be satisfied if church-related institutions merely provided a place for warm-hearted piety that would encourage campus ministry and mission trips.[14]

Short-term mission trips can be expected to reinforce questionable theology of mission in at least three powerful ways. In the first place, short-termers—especially teenager short-termers—are ordinarily much better prepared to make humanitarian

11. "Research and Statistics."
12. Priest and Ver Beek, "Short-Term Missions."
13. "Research and Statistics."
14. Dockery and George, *Great Tradition*, 88.

contributions of one kind or another than they are to make significant evangelistic contributions, especially in unfamiliar cultures.[15] Ministry choices are therefore limited from the beginning and without a great deal of discussion and prayer.

In the second place, short-term procedures most usually avoid one of the primary questions that have plagued church and missions for many years. *Namely, what is the mission of the church?* Nevertheless, they implicitly answer that question. After all, we are planning short-term *missions* and sending short-term *missionaries* who will be helping people "in Jesus's name"—what is that if not *mission*? The upshot is that, in America alone, annually from one to two million short-termers—often among the youngest and least prepared—have been reinforcing a holistic interpretation of mission by reporting all the good things they have been able to do in Jesus's name!

In the third place (and in addition to the piety of the Praise movement as I have suggested), it is often the "warm-hearted piety" of church-related institutions and not rock-solid mission theology that results in mission trips, as Dockery and George imply. The type of piety embraced by the Praise movement is reinforced regularly by short-term teams and their leaders whether they or we are aware of it or not.

Roland Allen's *Missionary Methods: St. Paul's or Ours?*

I had known and read Roland Allen's classic book *Missionary Methods: St. Paul's or Ours?* quite early in my student years but I missed its main message until much later. According to Lesslie Newbigin in his foreword to the 1961 edition of Allen's work, it never was Allen's intention to convince missionaries of the rightness of this or that missionary "method" but, rather, to urge "*the resubmission*

15. I refer here to short-term mission work as ordinarily carried on by Protestant Christians. As already indicated in connection with Southern Baptist mission (see p. 76) and should be noted in connection with short-term programs such as those of Mormons, the case would be different.

in each generation of the traditions of men to the Word and Spirit of God."[16] Quoting Allen, Newbigin continues: "There are no 'methods' here which will 'work' if they are 'applied.' There is a summons to everyone who will hear to submit inherited patterns of Church life to the searching scrutiny of the Spirit."[17]

When reading Allen's book it is easy to overlook that "summons" because almost the entire book is given over to a discussion of the strengths and, especially, the weaknesses of Allen's contemporaries as compared to those of the apostle Paul. That makes it seem as though Allen is simply promoting Pauline methods, while he is actually encouraging every generation to undertake the kind of evaluation he himself had undertaken and just completed!

It turns out that, in many respects, Allen's own generation of missionaries had been overtaken by the beliefs and behaviors of colonialism. Relationships, organization, missionary methods— even the content and style of preaching—all had been tainted and twisted by the colonial tradition.[18] How different that tradition from the attitude and approach of the foremost church planting missionary of all time—the apostle Paul! Allen writes because, like Henry Venn, Rufus Anderson, John Nevius, and many nineteenth- and early twentieth-century advocates of evangelism and indigenous church planting mission, he believed that the national church should be encouraged to assume responsibility for its own governance, support, and extension. Missiologists such as Melvin Hodges and Alan Tippett reinforced the same principles in the middle of the twentieth century but not until the time of Allen's death in 1947 did his *Missionary Methods* elicit the popularity it so richly deserved.

---

16. Newbigin, "Foreword," ii. "Tradition" in Allen has to do with the traditions that become part and parcel of the *modus vivendi* and *modus operandi* of each successive generation, not the great tradition we have been speaking of in this book.

17. Newbigin, "Foreword," ii.

18. Note that in using the word "tradition" Allen is not speaking of something positive such as the great tradition of Christian thinking. He is speaking about the tradition that had come to characterize the colonial mindset that had come to grip the Western nations of his day, including the United States.

Closing Comments

Evangelicals must work and pray together in resubmission of their ways of thinking and working to the ministry of the Holy Spirit. They must recover the faith of the fathers and the mission of the Revivalists. Nothing less will rescue American missions from a marginal role. Nothing less will reinvigorate historic doctrine and get missions back on the track to world evangelization.

I close with several well-thought-out and well-stated encouragements to that end.

Robert Duncan Culver's View of "A Greater Commission" and the Book of Romans

According to an earlier systematic theologian of TEDS, Paul's personal missionary mandate had two parts. The first part was delivered by Ananias at Damascus and, possibly, by some special revelation in Paul's own experience. The second part was a necessary inference from the whole Bible as it existed at that time. Instead of "As you go make disciples of all nations" (Culver's translation of Matt 28:19a), through the Holy Spirit, the Lord now gives Paul *and the church* a "Greater Commission" saying, in effect, "You go and preach the gospel to the whole world or else send others who will go" (cf. Rom 10:14–15). In these verses Paul posits a special mission—a "human sending."[19] Christ was sent into the world by the Father. The apostles were sent into the world by Christ. Christians are *already in the world*. They are to be salt and light and, as they go about in the world, they are to make disciples. *But, beyond that, there is a special "human sending" of and by Christ's people: namely, some must go, and those who do not go must send others.*

In brief,

> The people of the world are lost;
> They must hear the gospel to be saved;

19. Culver, *Greater Commission*, 119.

Christians must go with the gospel;
Christians who do not go must send others.[20]

Also according to Culver, Paul's letter to the Christians in Rome is mission-oriented from beginning to end. Paul begins his letter by writing concerning the truth and power of the gospel on the one hand, and the "sheer lostness" (to use Don Carson's phrase) of both Jews and gentiles on the other. He then offers scintillating synopses of fundamental doctrines having to do with the salvation of the lost—with the plight of all mankind from early tribal pagans, to civilized Greeks and Romans, and on to the Law-possessing children of Abraham. Then in Rom 9–11 Paul nests all of this in an overarching and divinely orchestrated missionary plan for which all believers should ascribe glory to God, and to the fulfillment of which they should present their body as a living sacrifice (Rom 11:33—12:3).

Finally, Paul deals with a matter that he had in mind from the beginning. Namely, a fervent request that the believers in Rome support his mission to evangelize the western Mediterranean as far as Spain (Rom 15:22–33).

The View of the "Dean" of Twentieth-Century Evangelical Theologians, Carl F. H. Henry

It would be difficult, I think, to state the mission and outcome of the Great Commission better than Henry stated it in his *Plea for Evangelical Demonstration*:

> To call men to their created dignity, to rescue them from sin's hell and death, to renew them in salvation's grace and power, to awaken their sense of eternal destiny, and to renew them in the image of God, the church gave herself in glad obedience to the Great Commission of her Risen Head, and *regarded fulfillment of this evangelistic mandate as her number one task in the world.*[21]

20. Summary of Culver, *Greater Commission*, 126.

21. Henry, *Plea for Evangelical Demonstration*, 64–65 (emphasis mine).

The Testimony of a Leading Southern Baptist
Theologian/Missiologist, Keith E. Eitel

Along the same lines, the founding dean (now retired) of South-western Baptist Theological Seminary's School of Evangelism and Missions, Keith Eitel—after reviewing contemporary mission proposals that call for relevance but with little or no gospel proc-lamation, and for missionary service without concern for souls, as woefully inadequate—encourages evangelicals everywhere, saying, "Let us reaffirm the Great Commission and tell the old, old story to everyone who wills to listen."[22]

22. Eitel, "On Becoming Missional," 38.

Postscript

MY WIFE, GERTRUDE, AND I were privileged to be in the company of several TEDS faculty couples at the Kantzer home in Highland Park when the Kantzers and Carl Henry met for the last time. It was the day before the Kantzers were scheduled to depart Illinois and head for their retirement home in Connecticut. Henry had journeyed from his home in southern Wisconsin to bid what turned out to be a final farewell to his longtime friends and Christian colleagues.

At one point in the proceedings Henry requested that a box of books be retrieved from the trunk of his car. That done, and with the box beside his chair, Henry proceeded to tell of his concern for evangelicalism. He spoke of his experiences in Edinburgh after delivering the Rutherford Lectures several years earlier in 1989 and of the circumstances surrounding their subsequent publication here at home the following year.[1] Henry mentioned his disappointment that the book had not received the positive response hoped for and his concern for the future of Protestantism in general and evangelicalism in particular. Then he opened the box and holding up a copy of *Toward a Recovery of Christian Belief* said, "Brethren, take as many copies as you can profitably use. You are welcome to them. I have more in my car."

1. See Henry, *Toward a Recovery of Christian Belief.*

Then, as reminiscences melded into expressions of affection and gratitude followed by a final prayer of thanks for the past and hope for the future, these two giants of the faith parted company for the last time. One cannot have known them personally, worked with them patiently, and learned from them greatly without the renewal of confidence that their God and ours will work all things after the counsel of his will and, ultimately, bring complete salvation to his believing people and divine justice to our troubled world.

One Millennial's Response Essay

Lianna Davis

May 2018

ALL TOLD, FROM BIBLE college to seminary thus far, I have evidently been the recipient of a series of sometimes perplexing theological projectiles launched out of a timeline from 1976, the Year of the Evangelical (p. 73), toward 2018 with its "theological orphans" (p. 110).

Standing on Two Different Grounds

But the foreshadowing for my involvement in this project started even before my formal college and seminary classes. As a child, larger family gatherings were peppered with theological evaluations and car rides home from church invariably consisted, at least in part, of sermon analyses. As a churchgoer and a family member, the messages I heard were not all the same. My understanding of theology and biblical interpretation grew in a somewhat trepidatious position between two grounds. At church, I knew warmhearted brothers and sisters (p. 118) who taught the primacy of the Bible, while often emphasizing how to sense, feel, or experience God from it. In my warm-hearted family, I observed a tethering to the Bible (p. xvi) going beyond an emphasis of its primacy to demonstrating a right subjection to its authoritative, historically attested, and literal meaning.

Through those early years and through college and seminary thus far, I caught sight of—and sometimes took part in—prevalent themes that have been observed in this book. A biblical interpretation was typically warranted as long as it was heartfelt, could be considered plausible, and was corroborated by some variety of commentary—all making one's own "reasonableness" an interpretational authority, without consideration of the great tradition. Helping the poor and marginalized or passing along a kind gesture—a "random act of kindness"—to another person was frequently championed above or on par with evangelism of the spiritually dead. The presence of differing theological viewpoints was valued—"we all need each other"—above pursuing sincere dialogue aimed at determining the best exegetical approach (while I believe we need each other as people, Scripture has only one correct interpretation in all of our areas of theological difference, such that variances in interpretation cannot rightly be considered a "need"). Yet, from my family context, I understood the priority of the eternal in gospel proclamation, standards of carefulness in accurate biblical interpretation, and not only the ability but also the importance of pure-heartedly debating theological issues with those we love.

My two grounds started to become so distinct, and even dichotomous, that I could no longer keep my feet on both. Being a Bible college and seminary student, I valued sound doctrine and accurate Scriptural interpretation; yet, I understood only a periphery of the difficulties I had begun to perceive. While not apprehending how much I had (and have!) yet to learn—or perhaps not knowing how to admit it because I knew the side I needed both feet to be planted on (the family side)—I sought to secure help "for my peers" from my grandfather concerning the difficulties I had observed. Comical, I know. But that is when and why I first spoke with him about what developed into this project.

Hope about Choosing One Ground

As he and I progressed—reading through drafts of this manuscript and sitting for one-on-one teaching times through his material—I began to see myself a splash in various tides. In the meliorist one (pp. 89–92), how many times I had hunted for God in my feelings in order to be led! How many times I had searched for validation of my spiritual maturity in my senses of God—not hesitating to communicate the "authority" of my feelings about Scripture or my perceived leadings from God that came in my times of prayer with the Scripture to peers, as if the one with the most "feelings" had the greatest authority!

In practice at times and in the books I had been most drawn to, I saw myself in the liberal theologians who "contend that experience and feelings, not creeds or doctrine, provided the foundation of Christianity. The ultimate authority for faith was the self-evidencing testimony of the heart in the individual believer" (p. 53). I saw my "Christian" language reflective of the social sciences; for example, personality profiles have been nearly authoritative for how I have considered my and others' actions and responsibilities. I saw myself in those who are more interested in stories of what missionaries' activities have been, over and above what they have believed—in those who have not appreciated the fundamentalists' doctrinal and missionary contributions, though a graduate of D. L. Moody's namesake institute (p. 70). I saw myself in those highly intrigued with seeing Scripture first and foremost as story or drama (p. 102). I saw myself bereft of Scriptural interpretation authority (p. 92), unwittingly attempting to become my own both in writing and in church contexts. And I continue to discover myself in various errors.

Yet, I also learned more about how to choose between the two grounds and be secured, with a hopefulness that had entirely eluded me prior to this project. I see this theological and missiological hope through at least four elements I have learned in this book: the great tradition, a new kind of humility, inerrancy and the ICBI, and defying meliorism.

The Great Tradition

One afternoon, my husband, Tyler, and I made a trip to my grandfather's home in Rockford, Illinois. Though we were starting to understand the concepts in the book, "tradition" frankly had an un-Protestant and unbiblical scent about it to us. All together, we started by discussing our shared conviction about the importance of the Reformation to our faith. Then, my grandfather asked Tyler what first comes to mind when he thinks of the Reformation, to which he replied in effect, "*sola scriptura, sola gratia, sola fide, solus Christus, and soli Deo gloria.*"

My grandfather replied, "Now, what do you *call* that?"

An "ah-ha" moment came over Tyler and me. These phrases of the Reformation were not found in the Bible, but we were confident they communicated biblical truth to the extent that someone who did not agree could not be biblical.

I have been exposed to this new concept of the great tradition as an authoritative tether. The term "tradition" is only now starting to sound more familiar and less awkward. It is starting to broaden me from individualism, raise me from cynicism about the value of a history that once seemed to hold primarily disagreement, and inform my already-sought-but-unrealized desire to love God with my mind.

A New (to Me) Kind of Humility

From the onset, I was surprised that my grandfather did not use his own definition of "evangelical" for the purposes of this book.

And throughout the project, I noticed that he continually referenced Dockery and George, or various other scholars, on many points.

Having participated in the blogosphere that seemed, especially for an unpublished writer like me, to be a place for establishing oneself—I was not very interested in this practice of referring away from myself to the expertise of others, but rather in writing in such a way that I sounded like the expert. I do not simply mean that I lacked the integrity to refer to others in order to give proper credit—I could cite my sources. I did not recognize that if I am not an expert on a particular matter I am writing about, maybe—just maybe—it would be more helpful for others to hear from or be directed to someone who is. Someone who has spent countless hours of intelligent study and research to learn and discern what the Scriptures say.

This newly observed brand of humility stands in contrast to false expertise, a fault which I, as a millennial, have found especially entwining since the arrival of social media and blogging. It is an error I continue to find tempting because of the proximity of the possibility to my fingertips—I could hit "publish" to the blogosphere instantly while neglecting to write under proper authority by first doing outside learning and, then, gratefully referencing those further along than I am.

The International Council on Biblical Inerrancy

Concerning scholars and their work, I have learned of the activities of the International Council on Biblical Inerrancy. That fair, open biblical evaluation of a perplexing plethora of theological proposals in a way that brings wide consensus is possible and has been achieved in the recent past (p. 112) was astonishing to read of, and then, profoundly relieving. Having assumed all of history to be largely like present times—when it seems boorish to "presume" that I can be certain of much more than the basic gospel message and the practicalities of Christian living—I did not know such a possibility, much less a reality, existed. The theological accomplishments of the ICBI and its leadership continues to be highly intriguing to me.

Meliorism and the Doctrine of Inerrancy

After being grateful that inerrancy was defended against infallibility (p. 87), I read Dr. Vanhoozer's view on a traditional understanding of the doctrine of inerrancy as "divine information-processing" being "cheap"—creating "mere information processors" (pp. 100–103). Initially, I was taken aback because I had witnessed nothing like what he described in traditional inerrancy's adherents (I saw the opposite—an honor and reverence for the Scriptures and the God of Scripture that I would pray to attain.)

Upon further consideration, I saw no way around his theory of Scripture as divine information being cheap reflecting poorly not upon the adherents of traditional inerrancy but upon the information itself—how could *divine* information ever be cheap? Later, it unhappily settled upon me that I had not been giving heed to divine information as I ought—my meliorism revealed a propensity to think, indeed, that divine information could be cheap unless for my desired result.

According to p. 91, objective Christian faith is what "gives rise to" Christian living. So, I at first considered that, yes, if more time is spent on the former, the latter will be improved and the desired goal complete. But I now suspect that more change is needed within me, for if I pursue the objective faith solely for the sake of the Christian living—solely for the sake of the "hands and heart"—well, that sounds rather melioristic and cheapening of revelation. Instead, the only reason I should need to value and pursue the objective Christian revelation is that God has spoken it and has commanded it to be taught and heard (p. 116). That revelation, of course, commands all of me.

Learning the truth of the Bible, and then adopting that authoritative truth to inform my life in a way that compels Christian living is a newfound, blessed simplicity. I seek to continue to grow in this manner, such that the functional spiritual authority in my life is not my feelings or senses of God amidst my daily walk with Him. But I almost hesitate to write of the blessing, in order that I do not lead anyone else to make the same melioristic mistake as me—of pursuing the doctrine for the purpose of feeling blessed, or for the purpose of "feeling God," or out of any sense that "faith cometh by feeling" (p. 116).

With this meliorism I still most frequently find myself in error.

Concluding Reflections

My time moving from class to class could not be characterized by an understanding of the Bible through which all "Christians in every part of the world [or school] felt themselves to be at one with all other Christians" (p. 14). But then again, the great tradition has also never been taught to me as "essential" (p. 3)—or as authoritative to what God has taught about the lost, about missions, or about how to read the Bible.

As I have spoken with friends about what I have been doing, exactly, with this project, I have almost invariably said, "I am contributing my ignorance." Though my initial motivation was to help my peers, it is first I who have been helped. From my childhood until the present day, in my thirty-first year, who my grandfather is—that is, my firsthand point of exposure to these truths—has not changed. But my lack of humility and a typically millennial propensity toward flash judgments and being feelings-oriented, which so very often have set me comfortably as my own authority, kept me from hearing—from standing and working to root myself where I far earlier could have been.

Bibliography

Baus, Karl. *History of the Church.* Vol. 1, *From the Apostolic Community to Constantine.* New York: Herder & Herder, 1965.

Beaver, R. Pierce. *From Missions to Mission: Protestant World Mission Today and Tomorrow.* New York: Association, 1964.

Boreham, F. W. "William Carey's Life Text." http://www.wholesomewords.org/missions/bcarey7.html.

Cairns, Earle E. *Christianity through the Centuries: A History of the Christian Church.* 2nd ed. Grand Rapids: Zondervan, 1981.

Carpenter, Joel A. "Propagating the Faith Once Delivered." In *Earthen Vessels: American Evangelicals and Foreign Missions, 1880–1980,* edited by Joel A. Carpenter and Wilbert R. Shenk, 92–132. Grand Rapids: Eerdmans, 1990.

Coggins, Wade T. "Evangelical Fellowship of Mission Agencies." In *Evangelical Dictionary of World Missions,* edited by A. Scott Moreau, 332. Grand Rapids: Baker, 2000.

Crow, P. A. "The National Council of Churches of Christ in the U.S.A." In *Dictionary of Christianity in America,* edited by Daniel G. Reid et al., 798–99. Downers Grove: InterVarsity, 1990.

Culver, Robert Duncan. *A Greater Commission: A Theology for World Missions.* Chicago: Moody, 1984.

Dockery, David S., and Timothy George. *The Great Tradition of Christian Thinking: A Student's Guide.* Wheaton: Crossway, 2012.

Douthat, Ross. "Is There an Evangelical Crisis?" *New York Times,* November 25, 2017. https://nyti.ms/2jZOzfo.

Dunstan, J. Leslie, ed. *Protestantism.* New York: Braziller, 1961.

Edman, V. Raymond. *The Light in Dark Ages.* Wheaton: Van Kampen, 1949.

Edwards, David L., and John Stott. *Evangelical Essentials: A Liberal-Evangelical Dialogue.* Downers Grove: InterVarsity, 1988.

Edwards, Jonathan. "A Faithful Narrative of the Surprising Work of God in the Conversion of Many Hundred Souls in Northampton and the Neighboring Town and Village." In *Puritan Sage: Collected Writings of Jonathan Edwards*, edited by Vergilius Ferm, 163–219. New York: Library, 1958.

"EFCA Statement of Faith." https://www.efca.org/resources/document/efca-statement-faith.

Eitel, Keith E. "On Becoming Missional: Interacting with Charles Van Engen." In *MissionShift: Global Mission Issues in the Third Millennium*, edited by David J. Hesselgrave and Ed Stetzer, 30–40. Nashville: B&H, 2010.

Eskridge, Larry. "The 'Praise and Worship' Revolution." *Christianity Today*, October 29, 2008. https://www.christianitytoday.com/history/2008/october/praise-and-worship-revolution.html.

Fitzmier, J. R. "Beecher, Lyman (1775–1863)." In *Dictionary of Christianity in America*, edited by Daniel G. Reid et al., 123–24. Downers Grove: InterVarsity, 1990.

Fox, Frampton F. "A Participant's Account of Edinburgh 2010." *Evangelical Missions Quarterly* 47.1 (2011) 88–93.

Frizen, Edwin L., Jr. *75 Years of IFMA 1917–1992: The Nondenominational Missions Movement*. Pasadena: William Carey Library, 1992.

Geisler, Norman L., ed. *Inerrancy*. Grand Rapids: Zondervan, 1980.

George, Timothy. "Evangelical Revival and the Missionary Awakening." In *The Great Commission: Evangelicals and the History of World Missions*, edited by Martin I. Klauber and Scott M. Manetsch, 45–64. Nashville: B&H, 2008.

Greenway, Roger. "Calvinism." In *Evangelical Dictionary of World Missions*, edited by A. Scott Moreau, 155. Grand Rapids: Baker, 2000.

Grimstead, Jay, and Eugene Calvin Clingman. *Rebuilding Civilization on the Bible: Proclaiming the Truth on 24 Controversial Issues*. Ventura, CA: Nordskog, 2014.

Handy, Robert. *A History of the Churches in the United States and Canada*. New York: Oxford University, 1977.

Hanegraaff, Hank. *Christianity in Crisis: The 21st Century*. Eugene, OR: Harvest, 1993.

Hatch, Nathan, et al. *The Gospel in America: Themes in the Story of American Evangelicals*. Grand Rapids: Zondervan, 1979.

Hefley, James C. *The Conservative Resurgence in the Southern Baptist Convention*. Hannibal, MO: Hannibal, 1991.

Henry, Carl F. H. *Plea for Evangelical Demonstration*. Grand Rapids: Baker, 1971.

———. *Toward a Recovery of Christian Belief*. Wheaton: Crossway, 1990.

Hesselgrave, David J. *Paradigms in Conflict: 10 Key Questions in Christian Missions Today*. Grand Rapids: Kregel, 2005.

———. "Will We Correct the Edinburgh Error? Future Mission in Historical Perspective." *Southwestern Journal of Theology* 49.2 (2007) 121–49.

Hesselgrave, David J., and Ed Stetzer, eds. *MissionShift: Global Mission Issues in the Third Millennium.* Nashville: B&H, 2010.

Hocking, William Ernest. *Re-thinking Missions: A Laymen's Inquiry after One Hundred Years.* New York: Harper, 1932.

Hubbard, David Allan. *What We Evangelicals Believe: Expositions of Christian Doctrine Based on "The Statement of Faith" of Fuller Theological Seminary.* Pasadena, CA: Fuller Seminary, 1979.

Ireland, Jerry M. "Carl F. H. Henry's Regenerational Model of Evangelism and Social Concern and the Promise of an Evangelical Consensus." In *Controversies in Mission: Theology, People, and Practice of Mission in the 21st Century,* edited by Rochelle Cathcart Scheuermann and Edward L. Smither, 51–73. Pasadena, CA: Carey, 2016.

Johnston, Arthur P. *The Battle for World Evangelism.* Wheaton: Tyndale, 1978.

Jones, Robert P. *The End of White Christianity in America.* New York: Simon & Schuster, 2016.

Kane, J. Herbert. *A Global View of Christian Missions: From Pentecost to the Present.* Grand Rapids: Baker, 1975.

Kelly, J. N. D. *Early Christian Doctrines.* Rev. ed. New York: HarperOne, 1978.

Kirsteen, Kim, and Andrew Anderson. "Mission Today and Tomorrow." Edinburgh Centenary Series 15 (2011). http://scholar.csl.edu/edinburghcentenary/15.

Kucharsky, David. "The Year of the Evangelical '76." *Christianity Today* (October 22, 1976) 12–13.

Ladd, George Eldon. *The Presence of the Future: The Eschatology of Biblical Realism.* Grand Rapids: Eerdmans, 1974.

Latourette, Kenneth S. *Christianity in a Revolutionary Age: A History of Christianity in the Nineteenth and Twentieth Centuries.* 5 vols. New York: Harper, 1958–61.

———. *Three Centuries of Advance.* New York: Harper, 1959.

Leith, John H., ed. *Creeds of the Churches: A Reader in Christian Doctrine from the Bible to the Present.* Garden City, NY: Doubleday Anchor, 1963.

Lindsell, Harold. *The Battle for the Bible: The Book That Rocked the Evangelical World.* Grand Rapids: Zondervan, 1976.

Little, Christopher R. "In Response to 'The Future of Evangelicals in Mission.'" In *MissionShift: Global Mission Issues in the Third Millennium,* edited by David J. Hesselgrave and Ed Stetzer, 203–22. Nashville: B&H, 2010.

Longfield, B. J. "Liberalism/Modernism, Protestant (c. 1870s–1930s)." In *Dictionary of Christianity in America,* edited by Daniel G. Reid et al., 646–48. Downers Grove: InterVarsity, 1990.

Manetsch, Scott. *Trinity Evangelical Divinity School: The Early Years.* Deerfield, IL: Trinity, 2014.

Mansfield, Stephen. *Lincoln's Battle with God: A President's Struggle with Faith and What It Meant for America.* Nashville: Nelson, 2012.

McDermott, Gerald R. "The Emerging Divide in Evangelical Theology." *Journal of the Evangelical Theological Society* 56.2 (2013) 355–77.

McGee, Gary B. "Evangelical Movement." In *Evangelical Dictionary of World Missions*, edited by A. Scott Moreau, 338. Grand Rapids: Baker, 2000.

Moll, Rob, ed. "Engaging Global Reconciliation." *Trinity Magazine*, Spring 2011.

Moreau, A. Scott. "Consultation of the Relationship Between Evangelism and Social Responsibility (SCRESR) '82." In *Evangelical Dictionary of World Missions*, edited by A. Scott Moreau, 224. Grand Rapids: Baker, 2000.

———. "Putting the Survey in Perspective." In *Mission Handbook: U.S. and Canadian Christian Ministries Overseas*, edited by John A. Siewert and Dotsie Tolliver, 33–80. 18th ed. Wheaton: EMIS, 2000.

Naselli, Andrew David. "D. A. Carson's Theological Method." *Scottish Bulletin of Evangelical Theology* 29.2 (2011) 245–74.

Neill, Stephen. *A History of Christian Missions*. London: Penguin, 1986.

Neumann, Mikel. "Small Groups." In *Evangelical Dictionary of World Missions*, edited by A. Scott Moreau, 882. Grand Rapids: Baker, 2000.

Newbigin, Lesslie. "Foreword." In *Missionary Methods: St. Paul's or Ours? A Study of the Church in the Four Provinces*, edited by Roland Allen, ii. Grand Rapids: Eerdmans, 1961.

Noll, Mark A. *The Rise of Evangelicalism: The Age of Edwards, Whitefield and the Wesleys*. Downers Grove: InterVarsity, 2003.

Oden, Thomas C. *The Rebirth of Orthodoxy: Signs of New Life in Christianity*. New York: HarperCollins, 2003.

Olson, Arnold T. *This We Believe: The Background and Exposition of the Doctrinal Statement of the Evangelical Free Church of America*. Minneapolis: Free Church, 1961.

Origen. "De Principiis." In *Ante-Nicene Fathers*, edited by Philip Schaff, 4:766–810. Grand Rapids: Christian Classics Ethereal Library, 2010. https://ccel.org/ccel/s/schaff/anfo4/cache/anfo4.pdf.

Ott, Craig, et al. *Encountering Theology of Mission: Biblical Foundations, Historical Developments, and Contemporary Issues*. Grand Rapids: Baker Academic, 2010.

Priest, Robert, and Kurt Ver Beek. "Are Short-Term Missions Good Stewardship?" *Christianity Today*, July 5, 2005. https://www.christianitytoday.com/ct/2005/julyweb-only/22.0.html.

Reid, Daniel G. "George Eldon Ladd." In *Dictionary of Christianity in America*, edited by Daniel G. Reid et al., 627. Downers Grove: InterVarsity, 1990.

"Research and Statistics." https://www.shorttermmissions.com/articles/research.

Schaeffer, Francis A. *The Great Evangelical Disaster*. Wheaton: Crossway, 1984.

Schaff, Philip. *Creeds of Christendom*. Vol. 1. Grand Rapids: Christian Classics Ethereal Library, 2010. https://www.ccel.org/ccel/s/schaff/creeds1/cache/creeds1.pdf.

Scherer, James A. "Church, Kingdom, and Missio Dei: Lutheran and Orthodox Correctives to Recent Ecumenical Mission Theology." In *The Good News of the Kingdom: Mission Theology for the Third Millennium*, edited by Charles Van Engen et al., 82–88. Eugene, OR: Wipf & Stock, 1999.

"Statement of Faith." https://missionexus.org/statement-of-faith/.

Stevenson, William. *The Story of the Reformation*. Richmond, VA: John Knox, 1959.

Stott, John R. *Christian Mission in the Modern World*. Downers Grove: InterVarsity, 1975.

————. "An Historical Introduction." In *Making Christ Known: Historic Mission Documents from the Lausanne Movement, 1974–1989*, edited by John R. W. Stott, xi–xxiv. Grand Rapids: Eerdmans, 1997.

Stout, Harry S. "Great Awakening." In *Dictionary of Christianity in America*, edited by Daniel G. Reid et al., 495. Downers Grove: InterVarsity, 1990.

Sweeney, Douglas A. *The American Evangelical Story: A History of the Movement*. Grand Rapids: Baker Academic, 2005.

————. "Introduction." In *The Great Commission: Evangelicals and the History of World Missions*, edited by Martin I. Klauber and Scott M. Manetsch, 1–11. Nashville: B&H, 2008.

Van Engen, Charles. "ESSAY 1: 'Mission' Defined and Described." In *MissionShift: Global Mission Issues in the Third Millennium*, edited by David J. Hesselgrave and Ed Stetzer, 7–29. Nashville: B&H, 2010.

Vanhoozer, Kevin J. "Lost in Interpretation? Truth, Scripture, and Hermeneutics." *Journal of the Evangelical Theological Society* 48.1 (2005) 89–114.

Walker, F. Deaville. *William Carey: Missionary Pioneer and Statesman*. Chicago: Moody, 1951.

Walker, Williston, et al. *A History of the Christian Church*. New York: Simon & Schuster, 1985.

Wells, David F. *No Place for Truth: Or Whatever Happened to Evangelical Theology?* Grand Rapids: Eerdmans, 1994.

"Who We Are." https://missionexus.org/who-we-are/.

Wiersbe, Warren W. *10 People Every Christian Should Know: Learning from the Spiritual Giants of the Faith*. Grand Rapids: Baker, 2011.

Williams, Robert R. *A Guide to the Teachings of the Early Church Fathers*. Grand Rapids: Eerdmans, 1960.

Winter, Ralph D. "ESSAY 3: The Future of Evangelicals in Mission." In *MissionShift: Global Mission Issues in the Third Millennium*, edited by David J. Hesselgrave and Ed Stetzer, 164–91. Nashville: B&H, 2010.

————. "The Meaning of 'Mission': Understanding This Term Is Crucial to Completion of the Missionary Task." *Mission Frontiers Bulletin* 20 (1998) 33–34.

————. *The Twenty-Five Unbelievable Years 1945–1969*. South Pasadena: William Carey Library, 1970.

Woodbridge, John. *Biblical Authority: A Critique of the Rogers/McKim Proposal*. Grand Rapids: Zondervan, 1982.

"World Mission Conference Begins in Edinburgh." https://www.oikoumene.org/en/press-centre/news/world-mission-conference-begins-in-edinburgh.